William Pitt Palmer

Echoes of Half a Century

Poems

William Pitt Palmer

Echoes of Half a Century
Poems

ISBN/EAN: 9783744652537

Printed in Europe, USA, Canada, Australia, Japan

Cover: Foto ©Thomas Meinert / pixelio.de

More available books at **www.hansebooks.com**

TO

MARK HOPKINS, D.D.,

THE REVERED TEACHER AND LIFE-LONG FRIEND,

FOR HIS EARNEST ENCOURAGEMENT OF THE AUTHOR'S PEN,

AND FOR HIS REPEATED WISH

TO SEE ITS PRODUCTS IN A PRINTED VOLUME,

THIS LITTLE BOOK

IS GRATEFULLY AND AFFECTIONATELY DEDICATED

BY THE AUTHOR.

PREFACE.

THE author of the following verses frankly owns that he once indulged the hope of seeing them gathered from the various periodicals in which they originally appeared, and issued in book form ; but for a long time past, that pleasing vision had been dispelled by the stern realities of later life. He solaced himself for its loss, however, with the reflection that literary fame, like all other, is only for the favored few ; and even those with the highest endowments have been so anticipated by their predecessors, that they can expect to add but little that is rare or memorable to the vast treasury of original thought. Humbly accepting his just place among the innumerable inheritors of oblivion, he had ceased to remember the foundlings of his fancy, when the fond partiality of his kindred took in hand the task of rescuing them from their long obscurity, and of soliciting for their reunion such chance for further life, as their collected vitality might seem to warrant. He has called them echoes —audible visitants from the past—yet each with its own individuality. Should their mingled strain of grave and gay seem unnatural, the author begs to remind the reader that in the music of humanity the minor key is as often heard as its more joyous fellows. He gave voice, for the most part, to the originals of these echoes while toiling in the great city to which fortune had directed his unwilling steps, far from those rural felicities so vividly remembered, so inconsolably regretted, by the rustic exile to the strange artificialities of urban life. Should these reiterated regrets appear selfish and unmanly, he asks the critic to consider the depth of first impressions, the force of early habit and association, and the fact that there are creatures of the wild, utterly untamable by all the kindnesses of city or country. In justice to his honored publishers, he assumes the entire responsibility for reviving the awful echoes of the recent conflict. In themselves, these are now of little consequence, save as the current expressions of a very earnest and anxious patriotism ; and, in that view, may prove of interest to some future enquirer into the motives and passions of the late rebellion. Macaulay did not disdain to cull a wayside weed, even for history.

In conclusion, he truly avers that neither during nor since their frenzied enterprise did he entertain any but the kindest feelings toward all his Southern brethren ; save only the guilty few, who *would* rule or ruin the republic which had been founded by Washington and his immortal compeers.

CONTENTS.

CONTENTS.

THE CLERK'S DREAM.

———

THOU hast full oft been called Death's *brother*,
    Sleep !
  By bards whose fancy, as in visioned dream,
Beheld a god on every towering steep,
    Fauns in each grove and nymphs in every stream ;
But unto me, true MOTHER dost thou seem,
    Of life and beauty most divinely fair ;
Forever following Hesper's westering beam
    Along the weary haunts of toil and care,
    To shed celestial balm on all that languish there.

Yet souls there are so avarous of time,
    So sorely conscious of uncultured powers,
That, thankless for thy ministry sublime,
    They grudge the precious third of life's brief
        hours
From action lured to thy inglorious bowers,
    And lulled to soft perdition, blind and dumb !

Still for their loss requital fair is ours—
  Thou add'st by taking from the moiling sum ;
  Stealing the present hours to lengthen those to
    come.

Ay, let us ever gratefully maintain
  That thou prolong'st our being's little span ;
Bringing the buried years to life again
  As fresh and fair as when their lapse began !
The snows of age that bow the hoary man,
  Like ice-clad pine on hyperborean shore,
Melt at thy touch, and cheeks but now so wan,
  Resume the vernal bloom their boyhood wore,
  And in the desert heart glad fountains leap once
    more.

Behold yon guilty, hope-forsaken one,
  Whose grave yawns darkly for its felon prey
Beneath the scaffold, where to-morrow's sun
  Shall see the rude winds swing his lifeless clay !
Yet even *his* sharp pangs canst thou allay,
  O blessed Sleep, with thy most potent spell !
The phantom worm, the foresense of decay,
  Stern guard, and muffled drum, and dirge, and knell
  Evanish, as thy steps steal softly to his cell.

Man may up-pile the everlasting rock,
  And bid his fellow crouch unpitied there
Behind the bolted bars, whose closing shock

Shuts outward all but darkness, and despair,
And *thee*, sweet mocker of the tyrant's care !
　Who fold'st his victim to thy gentle breast,
And bear'st him forth into the wide free air
　　To paths that climb the mountain's sunny crest,
　　Or wind by fairy streams where night's soft
　　　splendors rest.

As thou did'st steal my spirit forth yestreen
　From clerkly durance of the long, long day,
Where through a rear, drear casement's latticed
　　screen
　A few shy beams of melancholy gray
Peered in on bondman woe-begone as they,
　Bending in silent earnestness the while
O'er figured tomes outspread in grim array,
　　From whose summed lore no wit of man could
　　　wile,
　With Momus' merry aid, the prestige of a smile.

Meseemed, at last, the cycle of an age
　Had passed since morning reinthralled me there !
And listlessly upon the leaden page
　My aching temple sank in sheer despair ;
When, haply, glancing at the casement, where
　A spider, monarch of the broken pane,
Spun round and round on his aerial snare,
　　I blest the fates mine eyes had seen again
　　One form, however mean, ungalled by curb or
　　　chain.

And as the creature glided to and fro,
  As if to shame the Helot bonds I wore,
The sickly glimmer grew, or seemed to grow,
  More pale and rueful dim than yet before ;
While the great city's jarring tramp and roar
  Of myriad hoofs and wheels in wild career,
Vexing the rock-ribbed isle from shore to shore,
  Receded gradual from my drowsy ear,
  And died into the tone of some far murmuring
    sphere.

At last, all consciousness of sight, or sound,
  Or aught that speaketh to the outward sense
Of life or form in this material round,
  Passed from my spirit utterly—intense
Oblivion drowned all waking cognizance,
  Till Fancy roused it to the magic play
Of scenes wherewith, in kindly recompense,
  She fills the void of sleep, as night of day,
  With infinite bright hosts where one alone has
    sway.

Methought a sweet voice wooed my drowsy ear :
  " 'Tis time the galling fetter should dispart !
Son of the Mountainland ! what dost thou here,
  Amid the painted pageantries of art,
Where truth lies dead in many a specious heart—
  Dead as the smothered germs that never more
Shall clothe with vernal green yon trampled mart,

Till o'er its wastes, as in the days of yore,
The deer shall bound again by Hudson's ruined
    shore ?

" Art thou aweary of thy narrow bound ?
    And swells thy bosom oft with stifled moan,
That yonder Sun, in all his annual round,
    Brings not an hour that thou canst call thy own ?
How few the charms thy city life has known !
    How cold the greetings of the bustling street !
Ah, in the human waste how vainly sown
    The seeds of future joys or memories sweet !
    Away ! and shake its dust from thy indignant
        feet !

" O, scorn to be the slave of Mammon's slave !
    Nor longer wear the miserable chain
That binds thee down in this unseemly cave
    From morn till evening brings her starry train;
Recording, cent. per cent., the sordid gain
    By keen-eyed Avarice in the market made
Perchance from his best friend ; while rang amain
    The loaded dice, and his keen smile betrayed
    How true he held the creed, that all is fair in
        trade.

"Thy life has reached the summit where the slopes
    Of three-score years and ten, converging, meet ;
The one, all gay with youth's enchanting hopes,

And rosy light, and myrtle arbors sweet;
The other, opening to thy pilgrim feet
  A dreary waste of deepening shade and snow,
Down which the posting years, alas! more fleet
    Than mountain torrent in its wildest flow,
    Shall sweep thee to the gulf that yawns for all
      below!"

Methought, obedient to the tuneful spell,
  I waited not the sibyl's second call;
Yet, pausing at the threshold, sighed, "Farewell,
  Farewell, old comrades of my twelve years' thrall!
Desk, high stool, coffer, journal, ledger—all—
  Ay, even to thee, Dutch chronicler, all face,
That from thy perch beside the dingy wall
    Dost seem to censure time's impatient race,
    And teach his flying feet the true Teutonic
      pace!"

Thus saying, down the gloomy stair I sped,
  And up the crowded street my footsteps bent;
The very stones beneath my lightsome tread,
  Seemed springs to dance me onward as I went!
No wild bird long in wiry durance pent,
  No sylph in rayless dungeon doomed to pine,
At last restored their native element,
    E'er darted forth into its shade or shine,
    With such a buoyant joy as then and there was
      mine.

Eftsoon behind me sank the giant mart,
　　By distance changed to semblant ruins gray ;
Unfelt the throbbing of its mighty heart,
　　Unheard the death-shriek of its last dismay :
Grim, voiceless, vast, the stricken monster lay,
　　The stunned earth crushed beneath its Titan fall,
Its stony ribs slow crumbling to decay,
　　Writing its fame in dust, and over all
　　The cloud of its last breath suspended like a pall.

But Nature rose before me fresh and fair,
　　Immortal beauty mirrored in her mien ;
Her brow unshadowed by a passing care,
　　Her bosom veiled in folds of purfled green,
And tranced in pure beatitude serene ;
　　The very ground seemed holy where I trod,
As if the trace of angels there was seen
　　Amid the flowers, that from each dewy sod
　　Looked up and sweetly blest the living smile of
　　　God.

And journeying onward with enchanted sight,
　　Erelong a wild and many-winding stream
Came dancing foward with a brisk delight
　　Across the green Elysium of my dream ;
Now softly shimmering in the summer beam,
　　Now coyly hiding where the plane-tree flung
Its shadow down unflecked by golden gleam ;
　　Yet ever singing light and shade among,
　　And this the fairy strain its choral Naiads sung :

Prisoned long in caverned fountains,
  Lost in dungeons ebon, eerie,
From the wild New England mountains
    We at last have broke away!
  Ours are feet that never weary—
See their silver sandals glancing,
As in moonlit mazes dancing,
    Trip we onward night and day!

Man, who minds not alien pleasures,
  Of his own forever dreaming,
Oft hath sought to curb our measures
    In the windings of the hills;
  But while smiling at his scheming,
Cheerfully in glens and gorges
We have wrought his sounding forges,
    Whirled his spindles and his mills.

Nature's myriad forms are proving
  That no thing was made to slumber;
All in endless cycle moving
    As the Mightiest has ordained;
  Hosts, archangel cannot number,
Walk yon skies with harps of gladness;
Why should ours, then, sleep in sadness?
    Why our flashing limbs be chained?

Onward! then, o'er foamy ledges,
  On! through groves of mirrored beeches;

Linger not to kiss the sedges
    Waving in the scented gale !
  Round the headlands, down the reaches,
Dance we on with murmuring motion !
Hark ! we hear thee, parent Ocean,
    And rejoicing bid thee hail !

Yet not long thy ravished minions
  Can be rescued from the fountains,
Whither far on misty pinions
    Winds that prowl thy stormy shore,
  Waft us to the cloud-nursed mountains ;
But, escaped their wildwood mazes,
We shall speed to thy embraces,
    As ten thousand times before !

Three days, methought, toward my distant home,
  Three nights, like days of more enchanting beam,
With heart as lightsome as its buoyant foam,
  I followed up the many-winding stream
That o'er the green Elysium of my dream
  Came singing onward like a pilgrim gay,
Who sees, at last, the sacred turrets gleam
  O'er Zion's hills or Mecca's deserts gray,
  For which his heart has yearned for many a weary
    day.

Oft drawn aside, as by a magic chord,
  Where green nooks slept beneath their own green
    sky,

I sat me down upon the margent sward
 And watched the laughing waves with pensive eye;
And, haply, if a flower came dancing by,
 I felt my heart with sudden joy expand,
And breathed a silent benison on high,
 For that fair token from my native land,
 Perchance that very morn pressed by some kin-
  dred hand !

Perhaps my mother's ! ah, what weary years
 Had passed away since that had pressed my own !
How many hopes all drowned in bitter tears,
 Like yon bright waif upon the waters thrown,
Had down life's swifter stream forever flown,
 Since that dear hand upon the parting hill
So clung to mine, as palm to palm had grown !
 And even now through all time's change and chill,
 I feel its lingering clasp, its fervid pressure still !

O when the bloom of youth's gay summer fades,
 Its zephyrs hushed, its music heard no more !
When age goes tottering tow'rd the wintry shades,
 That dark and darker wrap the waste before !
Dear Memory ! then thy magic charms restore
 The flowers that perished in the ruthless blast,
The birds that sang, the friends that smiled of yore,
 The scents, the sunshine round our childhood
  cast—
 Yea throng with Pleiads lost the midnight of the
  past.

In vain we seek the future to forestall,
   In vain we thunder at its iron gate ;
No warder answers to our yearning call,
   No Sybil turns for us the wards of fate !
A voice from out the silence bids us wait,
   And time full soon will ope the spectral hall ;
Yet gazing through the gloom with eye dilate,
   We see inscribed upon the awful wall :
   " Behold the end of earth, the last sure home of
       all ! "

Then let us seek not with delusive hope
   The future's starless horoscope to cast,
While lorn and lost amid the gloom we grope,
   Like dust of diamonds scattered to the blast,
Time's precious gems flash onward to the past—
   Ere we can call them ours, fled evermore !
Each fleeting jewel fleeter than the last ;
   But thou, fond Memory, canst the loss restore
   Of such as to thy shrine kind deed or purpose
       bore !

Yet never long might these soft pensive shades
   Beside the murmuring stream my steps delay ;
But stealing back to the forsaken glades,
   With quickened foot and pulse of brisker play,
Toward the Mountainland I went my way,
   Still tracing up the river's silvery line ;

And ne'er did wild bird in the flush of May
  Behold his native groves with brighter eyne,
  Or make their echoes dance with lays more blithe
    than mine.

For now familiar forms began to smile
  On every side, as with a fond surprise,
In one who piped so merrily the while
  A long-lost, grateful friend to recognise ;
The selfsame flowers that charmed my childish
    eyes,
  The selfsame birds that haunted grove and glen,
The same bright clouds that draped life's morn-
    ing skies,
  The same proud peaks that were their ramparts
    then,—
  All these in summer's prime were mine, all mine
    again !

As thus along the vista of my dream
  My careless steps their pilgrimage pursued,
Methought, far straying from the friendly stream,
  I came at last upon a terraced wood—
A steep, wild, labyrinthine solitude,
  That seemed all farther daring to defy ;
And as in deep perplexity I stood,
  Far up a cascade flashed upon my eye,
  And waved its snowy plume from out the very sky.

Well pleased the kindly summons I obey,
  And smile defiance at the frowning steep ;
Now up the crag I climb my clinging way,
  Now through dim coombs of matted laurels
      creep,
Anon o'er yawning chasms fearless leap,
  By wild vine pendent in the startled air ;
Oft from my foot the loosened boulders sweep
  With smoking crash from shivered stair· to stair ;
  Yet still toward the clouds with dauntless aim I
      fare ;

Nor pause to mark the upward distance gained,
  Or how the landscape broadened to the sight,
Till o'er the last grim battlement I strained,
  And stood triumphant on the topmost height.
And well, O Nature ! did thy charms requite
  The toil that won me thy aerial throne ;
Whence, far around, in summer's fairest light
  A green and glorious panorama shone,
  With all the tenderest hues to Memory's pencil
      known.

For not a form o'er all that living chart
  So wide unfolded to my raptured gaze,
But had its perfect image in my heart,
  Daguerreotyped in boyhood's sunny days,
Ere care's stern frown, or sorrow's deepening haze
  Had dimmed the glow of hope's celestial beam ;

Blindfold I could have thrid each silvan maze,
  Traced every wayward path and winding stream
  To shades where highest noon scarce wakes the
    owlet's dream.

All hail, I fondly cried, dear native land !
  Ye peaks that, frowning from your kingly seat,
Do bid the tempest's sounding legions stand,
  And furl their cloudy banners at your feet ;
Ye groves, where summer's gayest minstrels
    meet
  And charm the echoes with love's fondest tale ;
Ye hills, where flocks securely browse and bleat,
  Ye brooks, soft murmuring through the herded
    vale,
  Blue lakes, and golden fields, and peaceful ham-
    lets, hail !

O Freedom ! if oppresion's myrmidons,
  In after years, should forge for thee the chain,
And, o'er the bodies of thy lowland sons,
  Hunt thee from forth the strongholds of the
    plain,
Here shalt thou find thy sure and fast domain,
  Each crag a tower alive with glaive and gun,
And bosoms fired to teach thy foes again
  What valor ripens in the genial sun
  That smiles on Berkshire's hills and thine, fair
    Bennington ?

No tyrant's foot shall ever shame the soil
  Embattled round with freedom's mountain frieze,
And hearts whose pastime is the time of toil,
  Whose sorest penance-hour the hour of ease :
The willow bendeth to the passing breeze,
  In meek submission to its lowly end ;
While stands the oak with gnarled and stubborn
      knees,
  His flag aloft howe'er the tempest rend ;
  And they who share his hills, oak-hearted, bow
      nor bend !

What though the genius of these later days,
  With Science' grander lens and keener light,
Has touched Olympus with its searching rays,
  And shrunk its ancient deities from sight ;
Still doth their spirit haunt each kindred height,
  Shout in the whirlwind, dart the lightning's spear—
'Tis that which plumes the eagle's sunward flight ;
  'Tis that which whispers to the mountaineer :
  " Are not these rugged wilds than tropic vales
      more dear ? "

To me, more dear than all the world beside,
  Uprose again that long-lost silvan scene,
Surge over surge uplifted wild and wide—
  A billowy ocean, motionless, serene,
With green abysses winding all between ;
  While fleets of gorgeous clouds went sailing slow,

As loth to leave so fair a sea, I ween ;
  Trailing their shadows o'er the amber glow,
  That clothed with heaven's own smile the bound-
    less swells below.

But lo ! what form of fascinating power
  Amid the wonders of my dream appears ?
What dear enchantress in yon leafy bower
  So fondly dims my eyes with happy tears ?
Home of my chidhood's all too fleeting years !
  Do I indeed behold thee once again ?
O smile away thy truant's boding fears
  That thou, and all this fairy-like domain,
  Are but a trick of sleep—a mockery of the brain !

Nay, I will have you real, here and now,
  All forms on which these swimming eyes are bent !
Thou art Taconic of the cloud-crowned brow,
  And thou, the Mountain of the Monument,
Cloven in twain, and one-half headlong sent
  Adown the vale whence erst its grandeur clomb ;
And Greylock thou, that like archangel's tent
  Purplest the northward sky with thy great dome—
  I know ye, each and all, and feel that this is home !

Old friends ! the love that greets you is unchanged,
  As ye who smile to welcome me again ;
Long years have passed since boyhood blithely
    ranged
  Your realm from peak to peak, from glen to glen :

Far hence my bark amid the tides of men
　Has drifted helpless, compassless, and frail,
The sport of chance ; yet felt I even then,
　When skies were darkest, most adverse the gale,
　That here benignant fate would furl its weary sail.

Ye were the last to linger on my gaze,
　When fortune lured my thoughtless youth astray ;
As now the first your beacon brows to raise
　Far off amid the azure cope of day,
To guide and cheer the wanderer's homeward
　　　way ;
　And though with bending form and visage wan,
And brown locks thickly shot with early gray,
　He turns to where his blithesome steps began,
　The boy's true, loving heart still nerves the way-
　　　worn man.

The light reflected from thy glorious brow,
　Imperial Greylock ! o'er a thousand hills,
Steals with a softer splendor on me now,
　With tenderer warmth my languid bosom thrills,
Than when attracted by the fame that fills
　Far-listening vales, a wondering youth I came,
And at the feet of thy Gamaliels
　Sat lowly down, with that becoming shame
　Such presence needs must wake to sense of
　　　noblest aim.

O happy fate that led me to thy shrine,
  Dear Alma Mater of the fond caress!
How like a brimming chalice of glad wine
  My heart ran over with the bright excess
Of wondrous, inexpressive joyousness,
  As knowledge opened to my eager eyes
Her priceless record of all sciences
  Wrung from the mystic earth, the blazoned skies,
  And that sublimer realm within the Soul that lies.

O studious days! so cloudless and serene,
  Elysium's very skies seemed bending o'er
A vale of earth, reflected in the sheen,
  Its purple peaks and gorgeous sunsets wore;
And fairer yet, in eyes that evermore
  Grew brighter, watching at the Muses' shrine,
Amid the starry beams of ancient lore;
  Till o'er the mortal face whereon they shine,
  Veiling its clay, there steals an effluence divine!

Yet, Nature, glorious as thy presence is
  Amid these sunward peaks and dim defiles,
I must not let these wakened memories
  Enchant me longer with their witching wiles;
For lo! still gleaming from your silvan aisles,
  My gaze once more a dearer presence sees—
Thine, thine, sweet home! whose benison of smiles
  Falls on my soul from those ancestral trees,
  Whose green arms all the while wave welcomes
    on the breeze.

And who shall tell the joys for me in store,
  Though every Muse should smile upon his strain,
When, lightly stealing through yon cottage door,
  I stand upon its sacred hearth again ?
What arms shall clasp me in their loving chain ?
  What sweet lips, fondly vieing with my own,
Shall shower their kisses warm as summer rain ?
    What hours of soul-felt gladness shall atone
    For all the aching years to hopeless absence
        known ?

Swift as a page on blithesome mission sent,
  Away I darted down a near ravine ;
And soon the Mountain of the Monument,
  Whence I had gazed upon that lovely seene,
Towered far behind me in the blue serene ;
  Yet paused I never in my wild career
O'er sunny hills and murmuring valleys green,
  Till once again upon my raptured ear
    The sounds of home rose sweet as angel voices
        near.

But ah ! how cold are fancy's warmest dyes
  To paint the scene where absent hours expire !
The tears that tremble in the mother's eyes
  All lighted up with love's divinest fire ;
The calmer gladness of the hoary sire,
  Erect for all his threescore years and ten ;
The sister's irrepressible desire   •
  To cling within your circling arms, and then

The brother's cordial grasp, and welcome home
    again !

Oh, home ! where gleams of Eden still attest
    How bright and fair was love's primeval shrine ;
Such were the fond illusions that possest,
    At that glad hour, my dream of thee and thine ;
Each eye that turned so yearningly from mine
    To *look* its silent benison above,
Each faltering voice of tenderness divine,
    Each tear, smile, kiss,—how tenderly they prove
    That paradise unlost, where love responds to love.

Then spake my mother with sweet-chiding sighs :
    " Twelve years away ! indeed it was not fair
To leave so long before our longing eyes
    The painful presence of your vacant chair !
Vacant ? Oh, no ; the phantom of despair
    Usurped it oft, and gloomed on all around ! "
" But," smiled my father, " now that he is there
    Once more in his old place, let joy abound—
    The longer lost to hope, the welcomer when
        found ! "

" Yes," smiled my sister, " but the stray-away
    Must promise ne'er to part love's golden chain—
Nay, almost *swear*, that from this blessed day
    He will not leave us, even in dreams again ! "
" Thy cheek for Book ! " I smiled—" Yet oaths are
        vain,
    Dearest ; for, sooth, my wanderings are all o'er !—

Ah, be assured, the lessons learned of pain
  Are wisdom's oracles for evermore !
  I could not, if I would, forget their warning lore ;

" Forget that yonder world, so brave and gay,
  To whose bright scenes my dazzled steps I bent,
With all its promised joys can ne'er repay
  The loss of one sweet hour of home-content :
Ay, gilded world, the vail at last is rent,
  That masked thy haggard face and maniac mirth !
Henceforth my wiser years shall all be spent
  Here where life's morning memories had birth
  Amid the dews of love and sunshine of the hearth.

" Forgive the past, dear friends ! its hopes and fears
  Awake no more to sadden or deceive ;
Here shall the conscience of those wiser years
  Fondly essay past errors to retrieve.
Need I be sworn no more your hearts to grieve
  By absence ? "—" Nay," my sister smiled, " 'twere
      vain ;
For, truant, know we mean henceforth to weave
  Around your roving thoughts so fast a chain,
  You could not, if you would, break from its clasp
      again ! "

Conversed we thus, till midnight's brooding calm
  Around the vale its starry silence shed ;
Then, Oh, how sweetly rose the household psalm !
  How tenderly the household prayer was read !

Good night and happy dreams, how fondly said !
  As turning from the hearthstone's dying gleams,
Each to his waiting couch delighted sped ;
  Yet scarce to slumber for the haunting themes
  That charmed our waking thoughts like spell of
      happiest dreams !

Beneath my childhood's roof again I lay,
  In that dear chamber, lapped in peace profound ;
No change had passed its threshold since the day
  I broke away from its enchanted bound ;
The old familiar forms were all around,
  And each its own sweet charm of memory wore ;
And still the sweeter for the rustling sound
  Of boughs that kissed my casement o'er and o'er—
  How light their shadows danced upon the moon-
      lit floor !

Here was my favorite haunt in days whilom,
  To list the strains of Hellas' magic lyre,
Or hear its echoes in the harps of Rome
  Restored with scarcely less enchanting wire ;
Here had I first heard Dante's words of fire,
  And Schiller's wild and Goethe's wondrous shell ;
Here, too, had England's many-voicèd choir,
  All others drowning in its matchless swell,
  First taught my soul how vast the minstrel's scope
      and spell.

As thus, methought, withdrawn from waking ills,
  Though still awake, in that sweet trance I lay,
Morn swiftly rounded to her orient hills,
  And sowed them broadcast with the gems of day ;
Nor long they shone in garniture so gay,
  Ere I was bounding through their fragrant bowers,
Or down their dells, or o'er their lawns astray—
  What mattered whither led the dancing hours,
  Where every footfall lit on memory's clustering
    flowers?

This lake that mirrors half a league of sky,
  Was boyhood's ocean, where, in truant bliss
Oblivious, my merry mates and I
  Were wont to launch our span-long argosies,
Thread-rigged, and freighted with fair venturies
  Of shining shells or blossoms from the lea ;
Yet who so bold to say that he or his,
  Who bore the golden fleece to Argolie,
  Was half so proud of craft or blithe of heart as we ?

And hither, when its azure light was dead,
  Its dimples fast in winter's icy seal,
Aross the snowy fields we gaily sped
  To whirl and gambol on the giddy steel,
That gives to boyhood's bounding heart to feel
  The joy that danceth in the eagle's wing ;
And, when, at times, the ice-rift's sudden peal

'To shoreward thundered from our sidelong swing,
  With what a shout we made the upland hollows
      ring !

In autumn's sunny days, on yonder hill
  We shared the old bee-hunter's pleasant care ;
And when his murmuring guest had sipped his fill,
  And swift upwheeling from the fragrant snare
Glanced hiveward, straight as arrow cleaves the
      air,
  How oft, forth darting with impetuous bound,
We chased the laden plunderer to his lair,
  And made the distant woods reëcho round :
  " Ho! for the silvan mine, the sweet Dorado
      found ! "

And lo ! the stream that with such wayward grace
  Goes winding o'er yon valley's flowery breast,
As if it could not leave so dear a place,
  But ever wander there, a charmèd guest ;
Can I forget the pride my looks confest
  When first I swam its widest channel o'er ?
Or that glad hour of all my hours most blest,
  When from its swirling vehemence I bore
  The widow's drowning son in safety to the shore ?

And now I wander to the maple grove,
  That gayest scene of all the vernal year—
O what delight was mine again to rove
  Amid the silvan charms that clustered here !

The mossy troughs o'erbrimming, far and near,
　With sweetest nectar of the Dryades ;
The groaning sled, urged on with shout and
　　cheer,
　Toward the steaming lodge, that filled the breeze
　With clouds upcurling white among the budding
　　trees.

Such merry groups as wont to gather there
　From all the hills when jocund evening came !
Ah me ! the cards flew briskly in the glare
　Of cauldrons kirtled deep with ruddy flame :
No moping whist, but high-low-jack the game,
　Nothing the stake, and no wise Hoyle to thrall ;
Victor or vanquished, it was all the same :
　Nor mattered it to whom the deal might fall—
　The deftest rogue always shuffled, cut, dealt
　　for all.

And now the old red school-house rose to view,
　Where three lanes wandered to its green domain ;
And O what dear associations drew
　My footsteps thither o'er the silent plain !
Then, then indeed, I was a boy again,
　As, seated at my desk, I gazed about
On ink-bespattered wall and shattered pane,
　And heard, in fancy, that uproarious shout
　Which shook down showers of caps, " Hurrah,
　　boys, school is out ! "

But let me ever shun thy hateful banks,
　　Thou Brook, that babblest through the neighbor-
　　　　ing glade !
By me small meed of tuneful praise or thanks
　　To thy officious largess shall be paid :
Alas ! how oft, forlorn and sore afraid,
　　From some mad prank of boyhood's wild heyday,
Have I been sent to thy remorseless shade
　　For store of crimson osiers, whose smart play
　　Should leave my tingling limbs as rubicund as
　　　　they !

Nor far remote, behold ! the village spire,
　　Uptapering white in morning's rosy sheen,
Invites me on, and wings the fond desire
　　To muse once more in memory's holiest scene ;
And soon, where over mounds of deepest green
　　The sweet acacia's snowy blooms are shed,
I wander, lost in pensive thought serene ;
　　Stealing from tomb to tomb with silent tread
　　Along thy voiceless streets, pale City of the Dead !

And well may he who visits thy sad halls
　　Move softly, as with reverential fears ;
Where at each turn some graven name recalls
　　The lost companion of his joyous years ;
Where every turf the dew of loving tears
　　Has hallowed, even though it fold the unjust ;
Where every flower, its sacred form that rears

To win and seal affection's trembling trust
With its sweet-messaged lips, is born of human
    dust !

For lo ! these precincts have been hallowed ground,
  The bourne of life, for centuries untold :
Hither from all the forest wilds around,
  The red men came and scooped the yellow mould,
And laid therein the brave and sachem bold,
  Whom death had summoned from their scarry
    band,
With war-club grasped by fingers stark and cold,
  And bow, and shaft, and tomahawk at hand,
  Wherewith their parted shades might roam the
    spirit-land.

Ay, and two hundred years their flight have sped,
  Since they who wandered from the eastern seas
Inland to this far vale, have laid their dead
  To slumber 'neath these venerable trees,
Where sleep the dark woods' red autochthones,
  In blest oblivion of the restless race
Whose voice has swept their echoes from the
    breeze—
  Whose graves will soon their mouldering bones
    displace,
  Nor leave of them and theirs a record or a trace !

Even now, where'er amid these leafy glooms
  From side to side my lingering gaze I turn,

Each verdant walk is white with marble tombs
  Adorned with tablet, cross, or sculptured urn,
Where all, who will, the name and fame may learn
  Of those who sleep the dreamless sleep below—
The loved and lost, for whom the hamlets yearn,
    Yet not as those, whose tears of anguish flow
    From eyes that see no light, in blind and hope-
      less woe.

Ah, no ! not such were wont to be the tears
  By Edwards' followers o'er their lost ones shed ;
Nor theirs, whom Edwards' friend for sixty years
  Toward the land of silence gently led ;
And fed their souls with everlasting bread,
  Which whoso eats, shall never hunger more ;
And taught the mourner, blessed are the dead
    Who die in Christ, for, toil and travail o'er,
    Their works do follow them to glory's peaceful
      shore !

Whither thou wentest in thy prime of years,
  Dear Isabelle ! whose grave is at my side—
Hope was indeed the Iris of our tears,
  For well we deemed no sorrow could betide
A soul so near to seraph ones allied—
    To whom so much of beauty had been given,
That, had some far-returning angel spied
    Thy kindred form here gliding, morn or even,
    He could not choose but ask : " Sister, what news
      from heaven ? "

As thus involved in fancy's charmèd maze,
  Through dreamland's bright Elysium I strayed,
And heard the voices dear of early days,
  And mused by lake and stream, by hill and
    glade—
Wherever boyhood mid the flowers had made,
  Of old, a haunt unclouded by a care—
Sudden, methought, my pensive steps were stayed,
  As pealed a knell upon the startled air,
  And, springing to my feet, I woke, and found
    me—where ?

Alas ! not pacing o'er my native hills,
  Beneath the glories of the new-born day ;
Nor where the wanderer's heart with rapture
    thrills
  To see the smiles of home around him play—
Ah, no ! that vanished home was far away
  O'er many an azure league of mount and plain !
In *spirit* only had I been astray ;
  And thus recalled from slumber's visioned reign,
  I woke, alas ! the slave of Mammon's slave
    again.

Around, instead of morning's rosy sheen,
  The shadows fell of night's descending pall ;
There was the drear rear casement's latticed-screen,
  And there the comrades of my twelve years'
    thrall—

Desk, high stool, coffer, journal, ledger—all !—
   Yet ah ! how oft my bosom shall expand
With joy, O gracious Sleep ! as I recall
   The hours when thou didst take me by the
     hand
   And lead my spirit back unto the Mountainland !

Therefore, Enchantress dear, will I maintain
   That thou dost broaden, brighten life's brief
     span,
Bringing the buried years to light again
   As fresh and fair as when their course began !
Thou mak'st the man a child, the child a man ;
   Crownest the beggar, strik'st the king aghast ;
Unstayed by time and space, by bond or ban,
   Thou dost the future's mysteries forecast,
   And light with all its stars the midnight of the
     past !

PASS ON, RELENTLESS WORLD.

O World ! World ! World !
—*Shak.*

PASS on, relentless world !
  With all thy gairish pageantry and noise,
Pennon, and plume, and oriflamme unfurled—
  I envy not thy toys ;
For thoughts that sting the brain,
  On that dark brow are registered in guilt ;
And thy poor heart is wrung with many a pain,
  Smile, maniac, as thou wilt.

Thou of the eagle eye,
  In the red chariot of conquest drawn ;
Cursed by the widow's and the orphan's sigh,
  Pass in thy triumph on !
Yet know, in this proud day
  Of exaltation and of victory,
There be, who, sighing, mark thy grand array,
  And, shuddering, shrink from thee.

Thou who, though woman-born,
  Art mortals' crowned or mitred deity ;

Pass on ! I shrink not from thy glance of scorn,
  Nor bend the abject knee ;
For though the Tyrian robe
  Wrap thee in hues as bright as Eden's sky,
And thy dread sceptre awe the subject globe,
  Death will not pass thee by.

Fairest and frailest flower,
  Beauty ! that joyest in thy heavenly birth,
Ruling all spirits with a witching power,
  Pass on, proud queen of earth !
Yet at no far off day,
  Shall fade the glory of that angel form ;
And near the bravery of its pampered clay,
  Shall lurk the darkling worm.

And thou, whose iron door
  Was never opened to the sufferer's cry ;
Whose stride to wealth was o'er the friendless poor,
  Unstayed by misery's sigh ;
With all thy millions speed,
  Insatiate, reckless of the trampled throng—
Justice hath yet in store the righteous meed
  Of thy inhuman wrong !

Traitor to friendship's trust,
  Who, fawning, smil'dst through fortune's sunny
      day,
But when thy dupe was stricken to the dust,
  Turn'dst from his woes away—

Pass on, dishonored one !
  Thy deepening shame, thy baseness go with thee—
There are dark spots upon the glorious sun ;
  Could earth, then, be more free ?

And thou, whose every thought
  Conspired the ruin of creation's pride,
Woman, for whom the demigods have fought,
  And Adam's noblest died—
Who, when her love was won,
  Didst spurn it for the wanton and the wine—
Pass on ! I may not speak thy malison,
  For vengeance is not mine.

But *ye*, to whom remain
  Unsullied honor and unswerving truth ;
Faith that our fallen race may yet regain
  The Eden of its youth—
Whose love for human kind
  Is ever active, patient and serene ;
Whose charities are like the bourneless wind,
  Unwearied as unseen—

And ye, on whom the call
  To wealth, rank, glory, has no mastering sway ;
Faithful, and just, and kind, in hut or hall—
  Oh, pass not thus away !
For sure it is unmeet
  That ye, who form life's beauty and its worth,
Blessing its mingled cup with all its sweet,
  Should lightly pass from earth.

LOVE'S SECOND-SIGHT.

FAR through the dim, lone vistas of the night,
  As eye to eye, thy form and face appear,
Love's inward vision needs no outward light,
  No magic glass to bring the absent near.

Seas roll between us. Lo, the palm-tree throws
  Its shadow southward from yon moonlit hill ;
And stars that never on my boyhood rose,
  Are round me now, and yet I see thee still :

Alone thou sighest on the beaconed steep,
  While sports thy sister by the waves alone :
Why dost thou gaze so fondly o'er the deep ?
  Ah, blush not, love, the tender truth to own !

I see thee sink upon thy bended knees,
  Yet not as one who bows in mute despair ;
Nor need I listen to the tell-tale breeze,
  To learn whose name is oftenest in thy prayer.

Thy cheek is wet—was that a falling gem
   From the pearled braid that binds thy golden
      curls ?
No, never shone from jewelled diadem
   A gem so bright as beauty's liquid pearls.

Thou turn'st away—though fair the moonlit main,
   No sail appears, thy yearning heart to thrill :
One long, last gaze, and on the night again
   Thy casement closes, yet I see thee still !

On thy sweet face, as in a magic glass,
   I see the shapes that haunt thy slumbering eyes :
What smiles of joy, when Hope's gay visions pass !
   What pictured woe, when Fear's dark phantoms
      rise !

Why dost thou wake, while yet the East is dark,
   To hold sad commune with the wind and surge ?
'Twas but a *dream* that wrecked thy lover's bark,
   Only a dream that sang his ocean dirge !

Even now that bark, before the homeward gale,
   Flies like a bird that seeks her callow nest ;
Soon shall thine eyes behold its furling sail,
   Soon thy fond bosom to my own be prest !

I could not fail to hold my course aright,
   Though every orb were quenched in yon blue sea :
Love's inward vision needs no outward light,
   Star of my soul, no cynosure but thee !

LIGHT.

Bright effluence of bright essence increate!
Before the sun, before the heavens, thou wert.
      —MILTON.

I.

FROM the quickened womb of the primal
  gloom
 The sun rolled black and bare,
Till I wove him a vest for his Ethiop breast,
 Of the threads of my golden hair :
And when the broad tent of the firmament
 Arose on its airy spars,
I pencilled the hue of its matchless blue,
 And spangled it round with stars.

II.

I painted the flowers of Eden bowers,
 And their leaves of living green,
And mine were the dyes in the sinless eyes
 Of Eden's virgin queen ;

And when the Fiend's art on her trustful heart
   Had fastened its mortal spell,
In the silvery sphere of the first-born tear
   To the trembling earth I fell.

III.

When the waves that burst o'er a world accursed,
   Their work of wrath had sped,
And the Ark's lone few, the tried and true,
   Came forth among the dead ;
With the wondrous gleams of my braided beams,
   I bade their terrors cease,
As I wrote on the roll of the storm's dark scroll
   God's covenant of peace.

IV.

Like a pall at rest on a pulseless breast,
   Night's funeral shadow slept
Where shepherd swains on the Bethlehem plains
   Their lonely vigils kept ;
When I flashed on their sight the heralds bright
   Of heaven's redeeming plan,
As they chanted the morn of a Saviour born—
   Joy, joy to the outcast Man !

V.

Equal favor I show to the lofty and low,
   On the just and unjust I descend ;

E'en the blind, whose vain spheres roll in darkness
        and tears,
  Feel my smile the blest smile of a friend :
Nay, the flower of the waste by my love is embraced,
  As the rose in the garden of kings—   .
At the chrysalis bier of the worm I appear,
  And lo ! the gay butterfly's wings !

VI.

The desolate Morn, like a mourner forlorn,
  Conceals all the pride of her charms,
Till I bid the bright Hours chase the Night from
        her bowers,
  And lead the young Day to her arms :
And when the gay rover seeks Eve for his lover,
  And sinks to her balmy repose,
I wrap their soft rest, by the zephyr-fanned west,
  In curtains of amber and rose.

VII.

From my sentinel step, by the night-brooded deep,
  I gaze with unslumbering eye,
When the cynosure star of the mariner
  Is blotted from the sky ;
And guided by me through the merciless sea,
  Though sped by the hurricane's wings,
His compassless bark, lone, weltering, dark,
  To the haven-home safely he brings.

VIII.

I waken the flowers in their dew-spangled bowers,
   The birds in their chambers of green ;
And mountain and plain glow with beauty again,
   As they bask in my matinal sheen.
O if such the glad worth of my presence to earth,
   Though fitful and fleeting the while,
What glories must rest on the home of the blest,
   Ever bright with the DEITY's smile !

HYMN TO THE CLOUDS.

Tum poteris magnas moleis cognoscere eorum,
Speluncasque velut saxis pendentibu' structas
Cernere.

LUCRETIUS.

ALL hail ! ye graceful children of the sun,
　　Whose genial beams evoked your fairy forms
From ocean's quickened bosom, or the lap
Of silver lakes, or heart of shimmering streams,
Or green savannas, where the moonlit night
Enspheres her brightest galaxy of dews !
Come ye with airy chalices to fill
The wild flower's languid eyes with tears of joy—
Come ye to catch the earliest smiles of morn,
And pour their reflex on the vales below ;
Or drape the closing chambers of the day
With curtains woven in the looms of heaven—
Come ye to hush the nations in deep awe,
As o'er their bended heads, in frowning pomp,
Ye waft the flashing armory of God ;
Or calm their terrors, when from deluged fields
They lift their suppliant eyes, and see again

The rainbow's promise beaming through the
    storm—
Come ye in gloom or glory, hope or fear,
Whate'er your aspect or your errand, hail !
Ay, ever welcome to the Mountainland
Where Freedom haunts be ye, divinest types
Of her embodied presence ; famed of old
To love the hoary fastnesses she loves ;
For there your grandeur finds its fittest throne,
And hearts to kindred majesty sublimed.

Wonder and glory of the firmament !
In earlier years strange questioning was mine,
Of what ye were, and whence, and whither bound ;
As to and fro your gliding phantoms trailed
Their slanted shadows o'er the sunny plains,
Or in mid-air slept motionless.   How oft
The half-conned task and tasker's dreaded frown
Were unremembered, as my schoolward steps,
Enchanted, lingered while I gazed and gazed
On your fantastic phases ! seeming, now,
Aerial mountains stranger than the shapes
That haunt wild dreams, or throng the fabling lore
Of earth's first minstrels ; then, celestial isles
Embosomed in the calm of azure seas ;
Then, bright pavilions where the storm-tost sylph
Might furl her ruffled wings in soft repose ;
Anon, sky-mountains cliffed with giant gems
Of ruby, sapphire, amethyst or pearl,

From whose resplendent peaks, methought, were
    hewn
The gorgeous shafts, and architraves, and domes,
That grace the vistas of the Fairyland.

Free rovers of the boundless and the free !
To every breeze ye fling your careless sails,
And course from zone to zone, by night or day ;
With store of laden jewels, to which earth's,
Thrice told in all their glory, were but dross.
Nor hoard ye these, blest almoners of Him
Whose bounty knows nor weariness nor bourne ;
But, true to your high mission, visit all
That breathe or be, with largesses of love.
To vernal climes, aerial argosies !
Ye waft from warmer skies the early rain,
And lo ! the lifeless bosom of the waste
Beteems with quickened germs ; the naked glebe
Is robed, anon, as with a mantle dyed
In liquid emeralds ; and every gale
That waves the bridal drapery of May,
Baptised in floral sweets, a spirit seems
Just parted from the Gardens of the Blest.

But Nature, most, in Summer's fiery reign,
Exults in your glad presence and adores ;
For then a deeper and intenser life,
And hopes and fears of mightier concern,
As linked with plenty's weal or famine's woe,

On your celestial ministries depend.
When faints the breeze, and e'en the very air
Grows visible with crinkling sultriness,
And flowers shrink earthward from the brazen
    gaze
Of suns that wanton nearer, day by day ;
When flocks and herds forsake the russet hills
For glens where nooks of herby green still smile ;
When upland glades are glorious no more
With flash of sunlit streams, and lowliest dells
Scarce catch the murmur of their dying dirge—
Then shouts the swain to hear the thunder-tramp
Of your roused legions, echoing from afar ;
And gladlier yet, to see their dusky van
O'erloom his near horizon, and frown back
The noon's effulgence from his withering fields.
Still, where he stands, so deep the breathless calm,
The spider's pendent streamer plumbs the air
Direct as line of steel ; but on the heights
Beyond the sultry vale, he sees the groves
Wave their green signals, and the harvest-slopes
Break into golden billows like a sea
Of amber glory, as the courier gale
Speeds onward in its heralding of joy.
Anon, the silvery curtains of the shower
Infold the lessening landscape from his view ;
And now the leafy shelter o'er his head
Rustles with liquid music, as ye pour
The beaded crystal from your misty urns ;

And hark ! the streams have found their harps
    again,
And, in wild chorus from the wimpled hills,
Proclaim their boisterous gladness to the vales.

And Autumn, too, rejoices when the storm
Unseals your wafted Horebs o'er her wastes,
And spring and mere replenishes anew,
To bless the homeless creatures of the wild
With grateful bounty graciously bestown,
What time all else grows pitiless and stern.
Nor are ye praiseless, when the ruffian hand
Of Winter strips from Nature's stricken form
Her weeds of faded wretchedness, and leaves
Her shivering bosom naked to the blast ;
For then around her palsied heart ye fold
Your fleecy mantle, till the sunny Spring
Shall bid its pulses throb with joy again.

Thus with the Seasons in eternal change,
And with the chainless winds, ye circle on,
O'er earth and ocean, through the day's bright
    round,
Or night's dim shadow, beaconed by her stars.
Oh, stoop your wandering pinions and upbear
A lowly suppliant in your flight sublime !
Yon mountain cincture of his native vale
Embraces all the universe he knows ;
Ah ! bear him hence to that remoter world,

O'er whose broad realms and intervolving seas,
Isles, lakes, streams, shrines and fields of old re-
    nown,
As chartered pilgrims ye have gazed at will.
Let him with you behold the morning-star,
While yet the mountain-peaks are palled in gloom ;
And gaze at eve upon the lingering sun,
While Alps or Andes mourn his vanished smile ;
Let him behold the eagle's stalwart wing,
Upsweeping, falter far beneath the height
Of your sublimer soaring ; and beyond
The utmost trace of man's determined will
To plant his foot upon the stormy poles,
Still bear him onward in your boundless sweep ;
That one, at least, of mortal birth may see
How ye for long dark centuries have piled
Their awful wastes with everlasting snows ;
And list the thunder of the meteor main
Boom on the shuddering air, when, many a league,
The frost-pang rives its adamantine deeps.

Vain wish ! though man may launch his echoing
    car
Sheer through the cloven hills, or bare the heart
Of rock-ribbed mountains for the glittering stores
Hid in their sunless crypts ; may mock the winds
As o'er the waves they chase his careless bark ;
Or bid the storm lash white the yeasty surge,
While, undismayed, beneath the wild uproar

He walks the pathless mazes of the deep—
Yet when his vain presumption would ascend
Your glorious heights, proud fondlings of the air,
The swallow soaring from her lowly nest
Doth laugh his vaulting impotence to scorn !

And yet the groveling worm—the meanest thing
On whose blind wants your blest aspersion falls—
Hath wings unfolding in its reptile frame,
And instincts ripening for a nobler sphere.
Therefore, O man ! though tethered to the clod,
Take heart from thy low brother of the dust,
And deem his fate presageful of thine own.
Yon sovran shapes, whose coursers are the winds,
Whose range the airy infinite, whose robes
The prismy texture of celestial beams,
But now were portion of the trodden earth,
Or of the weltering chaos of the deep ;
Till from gross ties emancipate, they rose
To nearer fellowship with sun and star.
Then lift thine eyes to those exalted ones,
And trust that when these Adams fall to dust,
The spirit, plumed for seraph flights, shall soar
To high communion with the hosts that range,
On Mercy's hests, the universe of God !

ORPHEUS IN HADES.

Manesque adiit, Regemque tremendum.—VIRGIL.
Geog. IV, v, 469.

Is this awful presence real ?
  This grim Pluto's dread domain ?
Or not, rather, some ideal
  Figment of a troubled brain ?
Nay, it is no mocking vision
  Born of frantic hope or fear,
And my heart with calm decision
  Whispers, Minstrel, be of cheer !

[Addresses Pluto.]

Lo ! the first of living mortals
  That e'er crossed the Stygian wave—
Do not spurn me from your portals,
  Nor refuse the boon I crave !
By that queenly form beside thee,
  Rapt from Enna's flowery fold,
King of Hades, do not chide me
  If I seem unseemly bold.

[To himself.]

Rocks and woods my footsteps follow,
   Wildest streams in silence stand,
When thy golden gift, Apollo !
   Melts in music to my hand.
Shall its tones prove less enchanting
   Here, than in yon world above,
When its master, faint and panting,
   Pleads the cause of life and love ?

[To his Lyre.]

Let me try what magic slumbers,
   Lyre ! in thy melodious chords ;
When to music's sweetest numbers
   Passion weds her tenderest words—
See ! the Furies lean to listen,
   Atropos relenting hears ;
Nay, e'en Pluto's stern eyes glisten,
   Proserpine's are drowned in tears !

[To the King and Queen.]

Oh ! how sweet your answer falleth
   On my spirit, rapt and still :
" Fate thy darling's doom recalleth—
   Mortal, thou shalt have thy will !
She for whom thy soul is yearning,
   Sunward shall thy steps retrace ;
But beware, the while, of turning
   Once to gaze upon her face !"

[To himself, enraptured.]

Shall I, then, again behold her,
   As in days so fondly blest?
Shall these widowed arms enfold her,
   These sad lips to hers be prest?
Oh, the just yet sweet confession
   Of a rapture so intense!
Silence were its best expression,
   Tears its truest eloquence.

See! yon golden gate discloses
   Glimpses of the blissful bowers,
Where immortal youth reposes,
   Crowned with amaranthine flowers;
And, as *she* the threshold crosses,
   From the fields of asphodel
Comes a swell of spirit voices,
   Softly murmuring, Fare thee well!

[To the friends of Eurydice.]

Sister Souls! your choral blessing
   Fate shall tenderly fulfill—
In my arms, caressed, caressing,
   She shall find Elysium still;
For, wherever truth and duty
   Link the loving, heart to heart,
Your fair world in all its beauty
   Sees its perfect counterpart.

[To the restored Wife.]

Grieve not, dearest, that thy lover
   Leads thee with averted face ;
Ah, the Stygian bourne once over,
   How he'll spring to thy embrace !
But till that dear consummation,
   Be the thought our mutual cheer :
That in deepest obscuration
   Each to each is ever near.

Lo, already, faintly gleaming,
   Far Avernus dawns to sight !
Down whose dusky caverns streaming
   Glance the golden shafts of light !
As they brighter fall around thee,
   Fainter pleads my woful vow—
Nay, though thousand oaths had bound me,
   I must see thee, here and now !

[Turns to embrace her.]

Fairest of all fairest faces,
   Oh ! the rapture, once, *once* more
To behold those dimpled graces,
   Lovelier far than e'er before !
But, alas, the hopes they waken,
   Vanish like a frighted bird—
Ah, so soon to be forsaken
   By a bliss so long deferred !

[To the opposers of his pursuit of Eurydice.]

Back, ye Gorgons, grimly glaring
  Where the rosy vision fled !
All your banded fury daring,
  I again will seek my dead,
Vain, vain boast ! forever vanished
  Is thy dream the loved to free—
By thy own blind passion banished,
  Justest Fates, too, banish thee.

Yet ye have not all bereft me,
  Parcæ ! spurned from Lethe's shore—
This dear solace still is left me,
  That I've seen her face once more !
And whatever hence betide me,
  That fair vision, day and night,
Like a star, at last shall guide me
  To her own blest land of light.

THE LAST AUTUMNAL WALK.

HEN we last paced these sylvan wilds, dear
    friend,
Each shrub, and tree, and swarded space between,
Were flush with balmy June, and every nook
Of all the grove could boast its own sweet lyre.
Our path was paved with shadows gaily flecked
With glints of golden sunlight, as it were
The print of angels' topaz-sandaled feet
Upon the glowing turf ; and as we strayed
From glen to glen, no dusky forms kept pace
With our own steps, along the browner shades.
Thy arm was linked in mine, and oftentimes
Amid the choral symphony, our lips
Broke into song spontaneous as the birds'

Four moons have run their cycles since we stood
In Summer's green pavilion, then so gay,
But now so changed we scarce can recognize
One form or feature of the faded scene.
No bird recalls the melodies of June,
No flower its sweets, no bough its rustling shades ;

Through all the roofless grove the sun stares in
With unobstructed gaze, and as we pass,
Twin shadows glide beside us, arm in arm,
With silent footfall on the dreary waste.
When now we pause, 'tis not with merry lips
To swell the sylvan concert ; but to blend
Our sigh with Nature's, as in funeral stole
Forlorn she follows Autumn's passing bier ;
And, dearest, while I turn to whisper cheer,
Thy blue eyes overbrim, and silver rain
Falls audibly upon the rustled leaves.

Yet know, sweet mourner, and assured, take
    heart,
That 'neath these russet cerements, not in death,
But quick quiescence, sleep the hopes of Spring !
No seed, no germ, no bulb of vanished flower,
No folded bud in all the bosky wild,
Is numbered with the dying or the dead ;
Nay, in the palzied heart of these stark trees
The languid pulse of life still patient beats.
A few brief months, and we will stand again
On the green summit of this forest knoll,
And list, delighted, to the flying harps,
That fill the leafy aisles with vernal joy.
Before our steps the velvet sward again
Shall spread its sun-flecked shadows, and full oft
By marge of dancing stream, thy careless foot
Shall sink in tufted violets instep-deep ;

What time the cornel and the hawthorn cast
Their snowy blossoms on the scented air,
And every floral chrysalis awakes
To life and beauty from its shrouded sleep.

Meanwhile, dear friend, in our suburban cot
Thy favorite flowers shall bloom the Winter long,
And day and night, with silent lips still breathe
Sweet-scented thanks to thee ; for in thy smiles
They shall not miss the charm of sunny skies,
Nor in thy household songs remember more
The song of birds, but deem 'tis Summer still.
Thyself their Flora, from thy genial hand
Shall fall the needed dews each coming morn ;
Till vernal sun and voice of vernal choirs
Shall call us forth to these dear wilds again !

TO A BUTTERFLY SEEN IN A CROWDED STREET.

WHEREFORE, little fluttering thing
   With the rainbow-tinted wing,
And the right, at will, to rove
Sunny lawn and shadowy grove,
Hast thou left demesnes so blest,
To be Babel's hapless guest ?
Here's no fitting haunt for thee,
Boon companion of the bee !
Born, like her, with flowers to dwell
In the sweet sequestered dell,
And at Nature's board to sip
Nectar from each blossom's lip.

Here, where neath man's iron tread
Earth's green beauties all are dead,
Thou wilt find no leafy screen
From the noontide's piercing sheen ;
And, at eve, no fairy home
Like the lily's golden dome.

Here, where hunger's eager pain
Pleads at plenty's door in vain ;
Or, if heard, too often must
Feel the scorn that flings the crust ;
Thou, gay rover, scarce shalt find
Chartered feast or welcome kind ;
For if man to man's austere,
What hast thou to hope for here ?

Haste thee, then, where skies are fair,
Fresh as Spring's the Summer air,
Bright as tears affection sheds,
Dews that gem the violet beds,
Pure as morn the perfumed breeze,
Sweet the sylvan melodies,
Soft the glow o'er hill and glade,
Cool the very noontide shade ;
And where all of earth and air
Freely Nature's banquets share !

" Hold thee, bard !" the bright-winged cries,
" Truce to rural rhapsodies,
Till I briefly tell thee why
Hither I came dancing by :
Seest thou all the vista gay
Thronged with fashion's proud array ?
Tinted silks, like Autumn trees,
Waving brightly in the breeze ?

Plume and wreath of brilliant dyes,
Rich as sunset's golden skies ?
Ruby, pearl, and emerald green
Basking in the diamond's sheen?
These are but my gloss and pride,
Tints and tinsel magnified ;
And where gaud and glare abound,
May not Nature's belle be found ?

" Mark again the motley throng
By thy side that sweeps along
With so gay and smiling guise,
One might gaze with wondering eyes,
For some sphered Elysium near,
Whence such shapes had lighted here.
Born when Fortune's starry scope
Cast its brightest horoscope ;
Heirs of leisure, wealth and will,
How should they their end fulfil,
But by idlesse, fancy, show,
As we rural minions do,
Whom they sometimes deign to visit ?
And both rhyme and reason is it,
That we, too, should not contemn
In our turn to visit them,
Nor ourselves unwelcome see
Where our kith and kindred be !"

MY FRIEND THE "FRIEND."

MY friend the Friend, of humble birth,
  Of sober garb and sect demure,
From all the tests of manly worth
  Comes forth, like tried gold, bright and pure.

The brow that modest broadbrim hides,
  With sculpture's grand ideal suits ;
And well the mind that there presides,
  Reflects divinest attributes :

A mind, before whose searching light
  The mists of doubt and error fly ;
As flee the spectral glooms of night,
  When morning opes her piercing eye.

But nobler far than noblest mind
  Impalaced yet in mortal clay,
The great, warm, genial heart enshrined
  Within that quaint drab cut-away.

A heart so prone to pity's throe,
  To angel kindness so akin,
The faintest sigh of human woe
  Is answered ere it well begin.

My friend the Friend you'll seek in vain
  Where fashion flaunts in noise and glare;
But try the haunts of want and pain—
  You will not fail to find him there.

Yet he, alas! for three score years,
  Beneath a grievous cross has bent;
But never weak, complaining tears
  Have marked the doleful way he went.

My friend the Friend—nay, Muse, be dumb,
  Or worth its noblest title give!
Remember Terence' *Homo Sum,*-
  And call him friend of all that live.

THE DOOMED SHIP.

GORED to the heart, still nobly strives
    The fated bark to foil the wave ;
As conscious of the precious lives
    Her shattered strength perchance may save.

Vain hope ! She sinks ! Nay, still she floats,
    For all her burden of despair !—
" Quick ! babes and matrons to the boats—
    Room for the weak and helpless there ! "

Not so, brave Luce ! But " save who can "
    Now summons to the desperate strife !
What weight has woman more than man,
    In the dread balance, life to life ?

Stand back, ye pale, dishevelled throng,
    Frail aspens of the ruthless sea !
Room for the stalwart and the strong,
    The bearded and the brave to flee !

Alas, when woman's feeble hand
  With brawny desperation strives !
Boat after boat, swift seized and manned,
  Flies with its freight of craven lives.

Oh, better die the martyr's death,
  At honor's call, by flood or flame ;
Than live to taint with coward breath
  A thousand centuries of shame !

THE SEA-NYMPHS TO THE DRYADS.

LINES SUGGESTED BY A COLLECTION OF EXQUISITE SPECI-
MENS OF ALGÆ.

Pontumque per omnem
Ridebunt virides gemmis nascentibus algæ.

—CLAUDIAN.

YE Nymphs! that haunt the sylvan stream,
    Or gambol on the flowery lea,
A dreary world, perchance ye deem,
    Is ours within the lonely sea.

But, sisters, leave your fair sojourn
    Of rustling groves and mossy caves,
And with your own charmed vision learn
    What beauty dwells beneath the waves.

Come lay your trustful hands in ours,
    And let us lead you, soft and slow,
To gardens graced with fairer flowers
    Than earth's most genial climes can show.

There shall ye see the purple palms
  That wave o'er grottoes paved with pearls,
And vocal with melodious psalms
  From the sweet lips of mermaid girls.

We've heard what floral beauty lies
  O'er all *your* world in vernal days,
Nor are your rose's scents and dyes
  Unhonored in our Nereïd lays ;

But fate has marred its queenly grace
  With many a disenchanting thorn,
And storms its tinted charms deface,
  And leave it faded and forlorn.

But come with us, dear Oread band !
  To *Flora's* ocean lawns and bowers,
Where thorns ne'er wound the fondling hand,
  Nor Winter blights their happier flowers.

Come where the callithamnian beds
  In vermeil beauty softly sleep ;
Come where the purple dasya sheds
  A Tyrian splendor round the deep !

Where, like a boundless prairie-scene,
  Broad fields of living cladaphore,
Out-stretched Hesperian isles between,
  Make green the deep's untrodden floor !

Oh, wisely have your poets sung
   That VENUS' birth-place here must be!
For whence could Beauty's queen have sprung
   But from our Eden of the sea?

EDITH.

INTO my quiet life there came one day
    A maiden on the April side of May ;
Such April as, by grace of kindly Fates,
Its brighter sister's charms anticipates ;
And with its buds half opening into flowers,
Makes us forget the bloom of later hours.
Shall I pronounce her beautiful ?   I could ;
But let me, rather, simply call her *good*—
A little, merry, artless, happy thing,
At whose bright smile the dullest cares take wing.

And after years of absence, passed afar
In those far climes whence springs our Morning
      Star,
With soft winds wafted o'er the Western main,
Into my life the maiden came again.
But *now*, the buds of April's earlier day
Were all in blossom in her perfect May ;
Yet if I call her beautiful, the blush
Of deprecation will her temples flush.

Well, then, to spare ingenuous maidenhood,
I'll call my Edith charming as she's good,
And pray the angels who withheld at birth
The infant wings when bearing her to earth,
May long retain them, ere at last they're given
To waft their sister to her native heaven!

THE HOME-VALENTINE.

STILL fond and true, though wedded
     long,
  The bard, at eve retired,
Sat pensive o'er the annual song
  His home's dear muse inspired ;
And as he traced her virtues now
  With all love's vernal glow,
A gray hair from his bended brow,
Like faded leaf from autumn bough,
  Fell to the page below.

He paused, and with a mournful mien
  The sad memento raised,
And long upon its silvery sheen
  In thoughtful silence gazed ;
And if a sigh escaped him then,
  It were not strange to say,
For Fancy's favorites are but men,
And who e'er felt the stoic when
  First conscious of decay ?

Just then a soft, cheek pressed his own
   With beauty's fondest tear,
And sweet words breathed in sweeter tone
   Thus murmured in his ear :
" Ah, sigh not, love, to mark the trace
   Of Time's unsparing wand !
It was not manhood's outward grace,
The charm of faultless form or face,
   That won my heart and hand.

" Lo ! dearest, mid these matron locks,
   Twin-fated with thine own,
A dawn of silvery lustre mocks
   The midnight they have known :
But Time to blighted cheek and tress
   May all his snows impart ;
Yet shalt thou feel in my caress
No chill of waning tenderness,
   No winter of the heart ! "

" Forgive me, dearest Beatrice ! "
   The grateful bard replied,
As nearer and with tenderer kiss
   He pressed her to his side ;
" Forgive the momentary tear
   To manhood's faded prime ;
I should have felt, had'st thou been near,
Our hearts indeed have nought to fear
   From all the frosts of Time ! "

"ARE YOU 'ROUND YET?"

WELL, yes, my friend, I'm still around,
   In spite of Fortune's cruel blows :
The weed, you know, oft holds its ground,
   In presence even of the rose !

Death seems to spurn or quite forget,
   At times, the meanest thing that crawls ;
The while his dart strikes down the pet
   Adonis of imperial halls.

Your blurted question doubtless grew
   From wonder, bluntly unconcealed,
That earth had not yet snatched from view
   This laggard to the Potter's field.

Am *I* to quarrel with the fate
   That spares me, howsoe'er abhorred,
And, with my own hand, antedate
   The severing of ' the silver cord ? '

I'm always fain my friend to please
    In aught that conscience may condone ;
But life is *life*, and its surcease
    The All-disposer leaves to none.

If I had made myself, be sure
    Some traits of worth should stand so clear,
That even *you* might still endure,
    Perhaps, my longer presence here :

For you should see me give their due
    To friend and foe, whate'er it be ;
And inly feel my debt to you
    Was always less than yours to me.

But let that pass—the world is wide,
    With room for all and courses meet—
The broad highroad for flaunting pride,
    The close, shy path for humble feet :

So we may go our several ways,
    Good strangers, near or far apart ;
For though the sky be full of days,
    Not one shall bring us heart to heart.

To you I leave the shining goal,
    So often won with honor wrecked ;
I fail, yet failing, will console
    My loss with unlost self-respect.

And so my simple faith shall rest
  In this fond hope, as aye before :
That some, though few, who knew me best,
  Will sigh, when I am " 'round no more."

ENVOY.

Friend ! though to careless, common sight,
A kind word, like the widow's mite,
    Seem but a worthless thing ;
In all the social marts of love
Its purchase-power is worlds above
    The coffers of a king !

LINCOLN, MARTYR.

NEVER for years, when, closed our closet
    door,
  In voiceless yearning we have bent the knee,
Have we once failed or faltered to implore
    Less for ourselves than thee.

For though our feet have pressed a rugged road,
  Where cares grow sorer with each day's decline ;
How smooth our path, how light our heaviest load,
    Martyr, compared with thine !

Perchance some shadow on our little fold ;
  Some golden expectation turned to dross ;
Some wanton blame, some summer friend grown
    cold—
    These were *our* sorest cross :

Thine, the vast burden of a nation's woes ;
  The fate of struggling millions, bond and free ;
To be upborne amid the frenzied throes
    Of hate and loyalty.

Thy pleading words for peace and brotherhood,
  Impassioned friends perverted or ignored ;
While foes their pathos madly misconstrued,
    And answered with the sword.

When steel was silenced in the fierce debate
  Of truth with falsehood, law with anarchy ;
Failing their country to assassinate,
    They turned and murdered thee !

Thee, whose great soul through all these stormy times,
  When steadfast reason from her moorings swung,
Sought but to save the merciless from crimes
    That palsied mercy's tongue.

All foulest names e'er coined by ribald scorn
  And linked with curses of demoniac hate,
Were wreaked on thee, oh, gentlest ruler born
    To freedom's martyr-fate !

Yet clothed in truth's impenetrable mail,
  That fears no wound from frenzy's fiercest shock,
These fell from thee as falls the shattered hail
    From the undinted rock :

And when the orphaned millions of the West
  Above thy bier their starry emblems furled,
The wail forlorn, that swelled from breast to breast,
    Went echoed round the world.

The grand, who watched with no benignant eye
　　Thy mortal grapple with despotic.pride,
Could not repress the soul's ingenuous sigh
　　　　When the great Tribune died.

And, till the prairie turf refuse to bloom
　　When Spring entreats it with her tend'rest care,
On all the winds fond thoughts shall seek thy tomb,
　　　　And breathe their requiems there.

"SO TIRED."

PILGRIM, whose path has been so hard and
     dreary,
  So thorn-beset, with clouds so overcast ;
No wonder, dearest, that forlorn and weary,
  Thy trembling limbs sink under thee at last !

"So tired !" Yet still, oh meekest of cross-bearers,
  How dost thou yearn and wrestle to be strong !
Not for thyself, but the beloved wayfarers,
  Whose heavy burdens thou hast borne so long :

Not through fair scenes of fresh and joyous
     beauty,
  With flowers to catch the foot on every sod ;
But wormwood wastes, forlorn as human duty,
  Since shut of Eden, ever yet has trod.

"So tired—*so* tired !" Ah, well, a blessed guerdon
  Is surely theirs who triumph in the test ;
When He who tries them lifts the mortal burden,
  And evermore the weary are at rest !

O, empires have flourished, and passed to the
  dead,
For whose glory the madness of millions has bled,
Since here, with a sway that no challenge has
  known,
The blue dome my palace, the mountain my
  throne,
I have reigned o'er the wilds from whose bosom I
  sprang,
A sovereign ne'er cursing nor cursed with a pang ;
While the years that have hurled the rent crag to
  the plain,
Have but lifted my brow o'er a broader domain !

A minstrel as well as a monarch am I,
And with green-harp in tone with all moods of the
  sky,
My matins first welcome the advent of Day,
As he springs from the Morn's golden portals away ;
And dear to his ear are the hymns I attune,
When in glory he looks from his palace of Noon ,

And mine his last smile as he sinks to repose,
And Eve's jeweled hand draws his curtains of
 rose.

Man shrinks to his covert on mountain and plain,
When bursts the wild tempest in thunder amain ;
But calm as the cliff-pinioned Titan of old,
I breast the mad onslaught, unshrinking and bold ;
Assured of my foothold, whatever the shock
Of the mad winds to wrench it uptorn from the
 rock,
And never once dreaming of triumph to fail,
When writhing, convulsed, in the grasp of the gale !

Yet the hero, whose locks shall ne'er whiten with
 time,
Whose bosom still throbs with the pulse of its
 prime—
Ever green, when my liege· groves are leafless and
 dead,.
Ever singing, when all their winged choirists are
 fled—
Even I, whose throned grandeur so scathless has
 passed
Through the spears of the lightning, the rage of the
 blast,
Must fall, and the osprey afar on the deep
Shall miss his green beacon that waved from the
 steep !

But the mouldering mounds that enhallow my
    shade,
Where the red tribes of old their great sagamores
    laid,
Shall grudge not a couch with their bravest and
    best,
Mid the gray cairns that grimly stand guard o'er
    their rest ;
And grand shall my fall be, my death-summons
    meet,
When far round the echoing mountains repeat :
"Room ! graves of the mighty—new honor he
    brings—
Let the dust of the kingly commingle with kings' ! "

PLEA FOR THE SPOILT CHILDREN.

DEAR simple Uncle Samuel, pray
 Let the spoilt darlings have their way,
  Just for this blessed once !
Why should you mind the old disgrace
Of making faces to your face ?
There's nothing mortal in grimace,
  Nor in their taunt of " dunce."

They've been so used, poor petted dears,
To storm and swear, for years and years,
  As whim or passion led—
To answer kind words with a blow,
Take no for yes and yes for no,
That if they may no more do so,
  They might as well be dead !

I grant they've had an awful spree,
Sown the wild oats of deviltry
  Broadcast, o'er sea and land ;
But what a harvest has been theirs !
What shocks on shocks of bloody tares
Insult the sower's blasted cares,
  The reaper's empty hand !

HURRAH FOR MEMMINGER!

MASTER–RACE! blest with superlative
parts,
You are not only peerless in science and arts ;
But you top the whole world in mechanical skill,
And of this the tip-top is your Memminger Mill.

Not a soul had a sneer for Fourdrinier's brags,
When he'd got his machine, fed at one end with
rags,
To gush, so to speak, at the other, meanwhile,
With a paper-flood flowing on mile after mile.

But whereas the Gaul grinds his rags into cash,
The Memminger grandly converts *his* to trash
So perfect, a ton of it doesn't begin
To pay for a tithe of the " stock " he puts in.

Yet, month after month, the blind Samson grinds on
From day-dawn to sunset, from sunset to dawn ;
Sublimely unmoved, though all Dixie assert
Each hour yields but sequence of sorrier dirt.

O boss ! of the grand rags-and-lampblack concern,
By far the best plan you can dream of, to learn
What's the matter the outcome's so wofully mean,
Is—to run *yourself*, bodily, through the machine :

For, though you may fail the Rag-Imp to discover,
You'll gain the advantage of being ground over ;
Or ground deadly fine, which were luckier still
For the dupes of your infinite Shinplaster-Mill !

THE SEER THAT DIDN'T SEE IT.

HERE was, once on a time, up in Utica
  town,
A seer of first-rate democratic renown,
Who, with eyes shut or blindfold, could see more, I
  ween,
Than by any light, anywhere, is to be seen ;
And he loved the dark veil from the future to draw,
That his " friends " might go snacks in the visions
  he saw.
With the scorn of that termagant Tarquin who rode
O'er the corse to whose veins her own being she owed,
He cries : "Look ye there ! Weren't it bliss to behold
That pampered New England left out in the cold,
To perish with all the fanatical fools
That ever were ' brayed ' in her infidel schools ?"

Then rolling his eyes, like an owl in the sun,
He groans : "Oh, my friends ! is it anywise fun,
To see that lean, awkward, unmannerly clown
Of the White House, his big foot bring squelchingly
  down

On our *Habeas Corpus*, *Free Speech*, and *Free Press*,
State Rights, and what not, on the plea of war-stress.
I'm a Seer, and see there is no sort of sense,
Rhyme or reason at all in this lying pretense ;
But the aim of a tyrant intent to crush out
Every vestige of freedom, the rail-splitting lout !
And proclaim to his serfs : ' I'm your Lord ! I'm the
      State !
Beware, for my *will* is the fiat of Fate ! ' "

Here blurted in Daniel of Binghamton : " Pooh !
You a seer of visions, Horatio ?—Go to !
Were there half of a mole's withered eye in your
      head,
You couldn't but *see* yourself verily dead ;
And had you the ghost of a nose, I'll be bound,
You would smell yourself ripe for a berth under-
      ground,
Where your relics, well-bedded in chloride of lime,
May, perhaps, cease to reek in the nostril of Time !
Lo, your friends at the door wait with coffin and
      bier,
Each an onion in hand to make sure of a tear
For the leader who had the inglorious lot
To bring his own hopes and his party's to pot ;
So, own you're defunct, make believe you're re-
      signed,
And let yourself sink out of sight, out of mind ! "

COUNTERFEIT PRESENTIMENT.

" What the Democratic Party needs is office."—*Tammany Oracle.*

E'RE sick to death of self-styled Demo-
crats !
Shams, make-believes of infinite concern
For the dear people's welfare, which, forsooth !
Lies just about as near the wheedler's heart,
As near the wolf's, the welfare of the lamb.
O that our ears had stops to close at will,
And balk the shameless wretches, as they bawl
Their hollow catchwords : Amnesty ! Reform !
Whose true interpretation is, *Our* right,
Vanquished, to rob the victor of his spoil
Won in fair fight ; to sink the Ship of State,
Unless the helm and freight be yielded *us !*
Our right to pardon perjury to God,
And treachery unparalleled to man ;
To crush the feeble, fortify the strong,
And, with a retrospective sympathy,
Condole with Cain for that fraternal blood,
Which, somehow, had befouled his innocent hand !

Men pardon him who tells the honest truth,
Albeit bluntly, and with slight regard
Whose self-love may be ruffled by his brass—
Who calls a crime a crime, a cheat a cheat,
If conscience bids him designate them thus :
So when the juggler says, " You see this sword—
Hey, presto, pass ! " and feints it down his throat ;
And when, anon, he slips it from his sleeve,
And frankly shows us how the feat was done,
A natural impulse prompts us to admire
Alike his candor and dexterity.
But when your Democratic mountebank
Belies his calling, and with saintly whine
Avers we look in vain to see *him* bolt
A mustard-seed with that small gorge of his,
The very while his epigastric crypts
Outbulge a boa's glutted with an ox—
'Tis hopeless hard to tell which most to loathe,
The creature's ravin or his brazen lie.
He love the people, he their rights respect,
Who picks their pockets while he pats their back ?
Who bids them shut their eyes and ope their mouth,
Then mocks their duped expectance with the shells
Of precious kernels he will share with none ?
Who lauds electoral purity with lips
Sordid and calloused with cajoling bribes ?
Who, when abroad, reviles Democracy
And all its hopes and aims ; in full accord
With haughty bluebloods, banded, heart and hand,
To prop the gilded dryrot of old thrones ?

Hear him still argue that "The Golden Rule
Stops short at Dixie, has no sanction there,
Nor ever had, where White is right and might,
And Black, full warrant for all tyrannies.
Ye that cry 'Kuklux,' have ye yet to learn
That angel visitants have graced the earth
Ere now, and scattered blessings in their path?
Our masking brothers are akin to these;
Shielding from harm the friendless and forlorn
Outcasts for color and the curse of Ham.
As for the Lost Cause,—why the Scripture smiles
Approval on the search for what is lost.
Then wherefore blame them, if they fondly dream
Of seeking, even by the flash of steel
And cannon-lightnings, that dear waif again?
In war they keenly hankered after peace;
Why not in peace now hanker after war?
Men are not mountains in their fixities—
No star that looks on any man to-night,
Will find him just the same to-morrow eve."

O charming Democratic paragons!
If you do crave return to place and power,
More than your country's honor and fair fame;
If you court office more than you abhor
Rebellion, treason, murder, perjury,
And all the lesser crimes that lackey these—
Why can't you muster manliness enough
To grace your greed by frankly owning it?

For pity's sake, drop all historic names
Bequeathed you by *true* Democratic sires,
For bright transmission, like the Gheber's flame,
Undimmed from age to age ; that so, while still
Ye grovel on beneath the patriot's scorn,
Your children may be spared the crimson shame
Of patronymic titles ; and, when dead,
Ye curse no stone with graven infamies ;
But sink at once to sheer oblivion,
Nameless and beingless for evermore,
As are the nothings of a dream undreamed !

SUMTER.

OUSED like a Titan from his sleep,
 The Northmen's gathered might
Frowns grimly toward the rebel deep,
Where Justice points the ruffian keep,
 And bids her thunders smite.

Vengeance has slumbered all too long,
 Unstartled by the cries
That tyranny can do no wrong,
Since might is right, oppression strong,
 And only treason wise.

Lord of the wild waves and the blast,
 Thy favor we implore !
Hold them in peaceful durance fast,
Till wrath's vicegerents leap at last
 Upon the guilty shore :

Then let remorseless Havoc rain
 Her red bolts, day and night ;
Till, like the Cities of the Plain,
No vestige of the curse remain
 Unwhelmed from mortal sight !

INVOCATION.

OH for Aladdin's lamp one little hour !
    To summon hither that prodigious Power,
Who never let impossibilities
One moment baffle his weird energies.
What would we do then ? This we'd say and do :
" Genius, forgive the task we put you to—
Unworthy your great stooping, we confess,
Save that the end redeems its littleness.
Away down South, the ' sunny South '—(forsooth !
So styled, because there's not a beardless youth
In all her land, but thinks, like Phaeton,
Himself could drive the Horses of the Sun
Better, a heap, than the great charioteer
Who's held the steady reins since time's first year)—
Down South, we say, 'mid sands and swamps un-
        blest,
The Fates have stuck a human hornets' nest,
Whose fiery tenants, ever on the wing,
Like Iö's gadfly, ply their maddening sting
On kith and kindred with exulting spite--
The nearer kin the wilder the delight !

Now, potent Genius of the wondrous lamp,
Whose might no mortal hindrances can cramp,
In pity rid us of the chronic pest
Of this excrescent human hornets' nest !
We grant its suicidal virulence
Would of itself soon end the foul offence ;
Yet wait not for that riddance to befall,
But pluck it up, sands, swamps, stub-palms, and
        all
Its buzzing venom ; and, as erst you bore
Aladdin's palace to the Libyan shore,
And set the foreign wonder on a site
Far down that land of chaos and old Night ;
So bear this native nuisance bodily
A thousand leagues across the tropic sea,
To some congenial Afric Ballyhack,
And let it never dream of getting back !
Hear us, O stalwart Genius, and obey,
And your petitioners will ever pray !

IMPUDENCE.

AS some brave bark her sails shook out,
   And slowly made wake from the crowded
      pier ;
Who has not heard the saucy shout
  Of the wherry lad merrily paddling near :
" Ship ahoy ! where's your line ? bear a hand, ho !
Why the deuce can't you, now, give us a tow " ?

And who has not seen the skipper's face
  Break into ripples, jolly fine ;
As, touched with some tickle of truant days,
  Anon o'er the taffrail he casts a line
To the loud little rogue of the tiny craft,
And, presto ! the eggshell is dancing abaft ?

But who ever saw, in his wildest dream,
  An Argo, rivalling Noah's ark,
With acres of canvas and Geysers of steam,
  Make for a pert Liliputian bark ;
And, dipping its proud pennon low, so low,
Humbly entreat to be taken in tow ?

Why, that is the wonder the world now sees,
  In the old Dominion *Valentine*
Made fast by obsequious F. F. V.'s
  To the scrub-palm dug-out, *Caroline ;*
And constrained to follow her, whithersoe'er
Liliput madness may please to steer.

Beware how you venture the Maelstrom's verge,
  Whither Secession pilots your way,
Or erelong the stress of its vengeful surge
  Will whirl you both down from the light of
      day ;
And your brag, and your rattlesnake flag con-
    sign
To the lowest deep of the world's vast brine !

A VISION OF DIXIE AND DOUGH FACES.

OO busy by day to go sauntering out
  To see what our turbulent world is about,
I can only assist at its night-ushered shows,
When in fancy they visit my attic repose.

And the strangest of scenes that e'er spell-bound
        my eyes
With a glamour of serio-comic surprise,
Was a vision of Richmond that rose yesternight,
Like a crimson mirage, on my slumbering sight.

For, as if just emerged from an ocean of blood,
Every object seemed stained with the horrible
        flood ;
While the clouds that gleamed red on hill, hovel and
        hall,
But deepened the hues which incarnadined all.

Of the crowds in the street as they jostled and
        swore,
Not a beggarly rag was undabbled with gore ;

But the focus that glared with the bloodiest hue,
Was the den where scowled Jeff and his Catiline
    crew.

And lo, while I gaze at this animate clot
Of murderers, perjurers, thieves and what not,
Such a ludicrous group at the threshold appears
As had made even Niobe laugh through her tears !

'Twas a set of forlorn Shaking-Quakers—in looks—
"Fernandy," Vallandigham, Seymour and Brooks ;
All shad-bellied, broad-brimmed, and meek as you
    please,
Each waving a thicket of dwarf olive trees.

And down plump they all on their drab marrow-
    bones,
As "Fernandy," the spokesman, in ruefullest tones,
Whimpers : "Take them, Great Jeff, though the
    bearers *be* worms,
And oh ! grant us peace on your own royal terms.

"In our bleak Northern hot-beds, 'mid curses and
    sneers,
We watered their slow-taking roots with our
    tears ;
And words can't express, as your highness opines,
With what toil we scarce got them through Lin-
    coln's grim lines ! "

"Avaunt!" yelled the conclave ; "make tracks for
    your lives !"
As they clutched their revolvers and flashed out
    their knives ;
"Do you think with *such greens* to tempt men of our
    brains ?
Ha! verdant peace-mongers, here's pay for your
    pains !"

And bang! bang! bang! bang! the red arsenal
    crashed,
As pell-mell down Shockoe the shad-bellies
    dashed ;
Skirts straight out behind them, chins ditto be-
    fore—
Of course I awoke with a side-splitting roar.

ENVOY.

Oh! yearners for peace, 'twere more wise to re-
    frain
From hunting the White-Winged in Dixie again,
Till assured that its Nimrods *yourselves* wont as-
    sail,
While crawling to shie the fresh salt on her tail!

JONATHAN AND JOHN.

Fee, faw, fum !
John Bull is going to come,
With cannon and ball and bomb,
To knock our towns into pi
And ourselves sky-high,
Because why ?
Why, because in one of his sea-chariots
We found two of our own Iscariots
Scaping unhung ;
And having of hemp no lack,
We ventured to bring them back
To swing as their namesake swung.
But the act has roused John's ire,
And, fifty times madder than fire,
He is coming to—don't, John, pray !
Your will we will not gainsay,
But let you have your way,
And the brace of hoary Judases,
Nay, *all* the brazen Theudases
That rebeldom boasts to day.
For you seem, John—excuse the mention—

To have an ancient propension
For a transatlantic traitor—
An indigenous Yankee hater
        Of kith and kin—
        Now don't begin
    To color, and stammer nay !
Do you think we've forgotten, zounds !
How you planked down ten thousand pounds
    For our Benedict Arnold, eh ?
And when you had bagged your prize
(If history don't tell lies),
    You found your royalty saddled
With nothing but Dead-Sea apples, and thistles,
Sow's-ear purses, and pig-tail whistles,
    And golden eggs all addled !
For the body and soul, for which you paid
Such a rousing sum in that West Point trade,
    Even Cockneys valiantly clarted,
Were of all human riff-raff the worthlessest things,
Save to show that the old saw squints shrewdly at
        kings—
At least at one Guelph—as it chucklingly sings
    Of " the fool and his money soon parted ! "
But *these* two Confederate traitors,
Pandemonian prestidigitators,
For whose reclamation, John, you seem about
To break the Bank of England out and out,
And send your last " lobster " to pot
With all your provincial sansculottes—

This brace of unparalleled Thugs
(Unlike the old dabbler in drugs)
Is worth all the cost your exchequer endures,
And the "lobsters" that go to the making them
      yours :
For Mason can teach even *your* aristocracy
A sneer as is a sneer at upstart democracy—
How to run human machines
With the least outlay of means—
And, John, if you'll place in his iron grip
A regular grand plantation-whip,
        This old epidermal afflictor
   Will do all the flagellation
   For the whole British nation
       Without one deputy lictor !
   And as for the *facilè princeps* of these,
   John Slidell Mephistophiles,—
(To say nothing of his involuntary knowledge,
Acquired in the paternal soap-and-candle college,
Where, without doubt, he became so very wise
In the concoction of all manner of lyes) (?)
He can teach how to swell a lean minority
Into a myriad Plaquemine majority ;
Can show young Bull how to eclipse the lustre
Of Morgan, Kydd, Cortez, or any grand old fili-
      buster ;
How to dwarf Catilinean perjury ;
How to excel in pocket-bleeding surgery ;
  For, John, you may cripple and blind him,

And he'll find his way to your London hells
Ere he's been an hour in the sound of Bow Bells,
And bankrupt their most magnificent swells,
   With one arm tied behind him !

BULLY FOR YOU, JOHN BULL!

THE schoolmen's donkey that stood stock-still
   Exactly between the two bundles of hay,
Whose equal attraction so balanced his will,
   He stirred not a hairbreadth either way ;
Mohammed's coffin, entombed in air
   Betwixt heaven and earth, a marvelous show,
Upheld by antagonist forces there
   In a weird, unwavering *statu quo* ;
The doater whose fondness was halved so well
   By the two gay rivals' buxom charms,
That which was the dearer he never could tell
   When both, at the same time, wooed his arms ;
The goodwife who looked with an eye so just
   On the grapple for life of husband and bear,
That which of the wretches should bite the dust,
   She hadn't the ghost of a wish or care ;—
All these are but shadows of Bull's " neutrality,"
Bull's unparalleled impartiality
Toward the belligerent Rebs and Yanks
      Pitted for mutual slaughter ;
The sweat and blood of whose slashing ranks

(Without the least squinting at thrift or thanks !)
He would stanch, good soul ! if he only could,
With the same fond zeal that the devil would
      The leak in a chalice of holy water !

But, John, though your meek, self-oblivious labors,
Prove you the kindest and gentlest of neighbors,
It wouldn't be strange if, sometime and somehow,
You found yourself caught in a similar row
To that your " dear cousins " are tussling at now :
And when, peradventure, you're fast in the hug
Of some grim Gaul, Celt, Caffre, Russ, Sepoy or
      Thug,
We Yankees, recalling the boundless excess
Of your zeal for our weal, can indeed do no less,
      In *your* mortal distress
(Being flesh of your flesh, John, and bone of your
      bone),
Than to build Alabamas to *let you alone*—
When you maunder for bread, to respond with a
      stone,
In the summary style that old Joab displayed
      When he found the young blade,
      By his love-locks betrayed,
A live target dangling adown the oak shade ;
And cried out, anon, with exuberant joy,
" Here's to you, my princeling, my high old boy ! "
      As he let fly a dart
      Right through thorax and heart,

And followed it up with another apace,
That the soul of the traitor might, haply, be
      eased
With a choice of *two* wide-enough outlets at least
        To take itself off into space.

Even so, my dear Bull, we are free to declare,
        If you do not beware
How you trifle with wrath that *not* all things en-
      dures ;
Yankee Doodle at last will, as sure as you're born,
Drive his shaft, barbed and baned, with unmerciful
      scorn
Through that cold-blooded, base hollow-muscle of
      yours !

DREAM OF THE DEMOS.

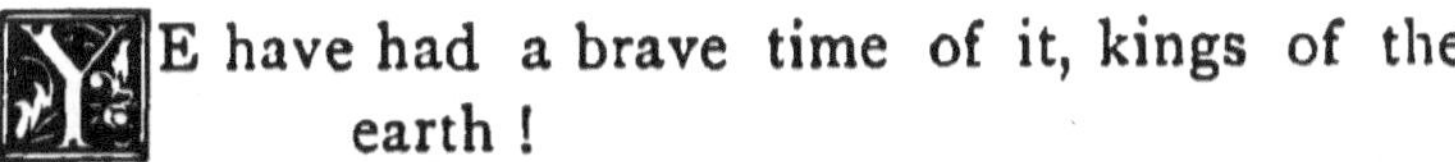

YE have had a brave time of it, kings of the
    earth !
  Since Gog first put purple to clay ;
And, dying, transmitted his wisdom and worth
To *Magog*, entitled by virtue of birth
  To lord it the right royal way.

And by craft ye've maintained what bluff daring
    began,
  Your grasp on the fairest and best ;
Consuming the cates, and commending the bran
To your equals in all that is noblest in man,
  As your consciences needs must attest.

We are told that of old there was one of your line
  So proud of his pomp, in the East,
That he deemed himself worthy of homage divine,

Till the Lord turned him out to eat grass with the
      kine,
    And grow a respectable beast.

Perhaps, by the year Nineteen Hundred or so,
    We Demos may come to such pass
As to rise and bid Messieurs Divine Right and Co.,
Czar, Bourbon, Braganza, Guelph, Hapsburg, all go,
    Like the great king aforesaid, to grass.

Then ' l'état c'est moi,' shall be ' l'état c'est nous,'
    The proud vaunt reversed for the nonce :
Having had quite enough of grand units like you,
We fain would just see how King Million would do,
    Both as sovereign and subject at once.

"WHO WILL THINK OF HENRY?"

HOW sadly strange, it seems to me,
    In these gay, smiling hours of Spring,
That mine the mournful task should be,
    Dear Friend, thy requiem to sing !

Thy younger years fair promise made,
    That when the pall fell dark on mine,
Thy fond regret should soothe my shade,
    As now my dirge would solace thine.

Full well I knew that *worth* may not
    To life's swift sands give slower fall ;
Yet ever, by thy side, forgot :
    Whom the gods love, they first recall !

As if, howe'er supremely blest,
    They could but look with jealous eyes,
On those to whom the summoned guest
    Had proved an angel in disguise.

Ah well, like breath of cherished flowers,
    That lapse of time but more endears,
The memory of thy living hours
    Shall sweeten all my coming years !

LINES TO A CHRYSALIS.

USING long, I asked me this:
" Chrysalis !
Lying helpless in my path,
Obvious to mortal scath
From a careless passer-by,—
What thy life may signify?
Why, from hope and joy apart,
Thus thou art?

" Nature surely did amiss,
Chrysalis,
When she lavished fins and wings,
Nerved with nicest moving-springs,
On the mote and madrepore,
Wherewithal to swim or soar ;
And dispensed so niggardly
Unto thee.

" E'en the very worm may kiss,
Chrysalis,
Roses on their topmost stems
Blazoned with their dewy gems,

106

And may rock him to and fro
As the zephyrs softly blow ;
Whilst thou liest, dark and cold,
           On the mold ! "

Quoth the Chrysalis : " Sir Bard,
           Not so hard
Is my rounded destiny
In the great Economy—
Nay, by humble reason viewed,
There is much for gratitude
In the shaping and upshot
           Of my lot.

" Though I seem, of all things born
           Most forlorn,
Most obtuse of soul and sense,
Next of kin to impotence,
Nay, to Death himself ; yet ne'er
Priest nor prophet, sage nor seer,
May sublimer wisdom teach
           Than I preach.

" From my pulpit of the sod,
           Like a god,
I proclaim this wondrous truth :
Farthest age is nearest youth—

Nearest glory's natal porch,
Where, with pale, inverted torch,
Death lights downward to the rest
                    Of the blest !

" Mark yon airy butterfly's
                    Rainbow dyes !
Yesterday that shape divine
Was as darkly hearsed as mine ;
But, to-morrow, I shall be
Free and beautiful as she,
And sweep forth on wings of light,
                    Like a sprite.

" Soul of man in crypt of clay !
                    Bide the day
When *thy* latent wings shall be
Plumed for immortality,
And with transport marvelous
Cleave their dark sarcophagus,
O'er Elysian fields to soar
                    Evermore ! "

LOOK ALOFT.

ADDRESSED TO A GIFTED FRIEND, TOO EASILY DISHEART-
ENED.

"Qui ose tout peut tout ce qu'il ose."—BERNARD.

IVE not thus to listless sadness
　　Hours the partial muse would claim ;
Up ! and with enthusiast madness,
　Storm the rugged steeps of fame !

Not by wishing, but by willing
　O'er the clouds to lift his flag,
Genius, aim with act fulfilling,
　Proudly climbs the laureled crag.

Did the youthful Swiss, long dreaming
　Europe's topmost round to scale,
Sit him down to idle scheming
　In the Arve's murmuring vale ?

No ; but o'er the glacier pressing,
　Up the granite's icy flank,
Step by dauntless step progressing,
　Won he, first, thy crown, Mont Blanc !

Be like him a bold advancer,
　　Nor the mocking laggard heed—
Upward !—from the summit answer,
　　" They who win may laugh indeed ! "

When the Scottish Jove's mad levin
　　Laid the noble minstrel low ;
Swifter tow'rd the muse's heaven
　　Rose he, strengthened by the blow.

He who launched at eve the thunder.
　　On the young aspirant's name,
Waked to see him throned in wonder
　　On the Himmaleh of fame.

Though than Newstead's bard less gifted,
　　Tune thy harp to higher strain,
And its voice for truth uplifted,
　　Shall a nobler audience gain.

Ask not, darkly musing, whether
　　Glory's dawn be far or nigh ;
Clash the flint and steel together,
　　And the sparks shall flash reply.

Chance speeds all, the weak assure us,
　　On or from the lurking shelf ;
Nay ! be thy own Palinurus,
　　Be thou Fate unto thyself !

THE ORANGE TREE.

FROM thine Eden of the sea,
  Hapless tree !
Where eternal Summer smiles
On the green Caribbean isles ;
Borne to this ungenial clime
In the scowling Autumn time,
Poor forlorn one, be of cheer,
  Hope is here !

Thou shalt find a friend in me,
  Outcast tree !
Who will bear thee from the storm
To a shelter snug and warm—
An asylum, Winter-proof,
When the snows assail my roof,
Or the sleet comes down amain
  On the pane.

New delights, in sooth, to boast,
          At the most,
Has our little plain retreat
In its unpretending street ;
Save a bird or two, a lute,
Pleasant books and nooks to suit,
And three pictures on the wall—-
          These are all.

Yet when rigor rules the year
          Far and near,
Thou shalt sit beside my hearth,
And its music and its mirth
From thy memory shall beguile
E'en the charms of that dear isle,
Whose far enchantment gleams
          On thy dreams.

For the haunt assigned to thee,
          It shall be
Just the soothest, sunniest spot
On the noonside of our cot ;
Where, through all the Winter day,
Little prattling ones shall play
'Mid the leafy shade so sweet,
          At thy feet.

So then, cheerly come with me,
          Exiled tree !

And beneath my modest roof,
Let thy greeting be a proof,
That to pity's arms and store
Lo, the peasant's humble door
With as wide a welcome swings
    As a king's !

KUBLEH.

LUMEN ET NUMEN.

WHAT beauty smiles from cloudless skies
  When night with twinkling lustre gleams !
Yet lovelier far, to these fond eyes,
  The light that from thy casement beams !

The Persian holds the East divine,
  And thither bows on bended knee ;
But in thy chamber's lighted shrine
  A dearer kubleh smiles for me.

How oft, when lated and forlorn,
  I've faltered on my darkling way,
That casement, like the glance of morn,
  Has filled the midnight vale with day !

Oh, fair the blush of orient skies,
  And lovely, evening's starry gleams ;
But dearer far, to these fond eyes,
  The light that from thy casement beams !

HANNAH DUSTAN.

SHORN of her stars, lone midnight broods
    O'er Winter's sullen sky,
Where through the broad New-England woods
    The stormy blast sweeps by ;
While from the mountain's jagged walls
The frost-heaved crag in thunder falls,
    Far echoing to the night ;
Startling the red fox in his den,
The roe-buck in the lowland glen,
    The eagle on the height.

Yet though no welkin beam the while
    Illume that gloomy scene,
Yon flickering watch-fire's smoldering pile
    Imparts a lurid sheen ;
Where, couched around its genial glow,
Outstretched upon the sheeted snow
    Twelve forest chieftains lie,
Wrapped in the brown bear's shaggy fold,
Their long knives gleaming keen and cold,
    As gleams the serpent's eye.

They heed not now the sullen scowl
  Of skies so bleak and drear—
The owl's wild screech, the wolf's hoarse howl,
  Fall noteless on their ear,
As there they sleep, toil-worn and grim,
With belted breast and scarry limb
  Red with the fresh scalp's flow,
Won when the white foe's roof-tree fell
With fiery crash and fiendish yell
  And shrieks of mortal woe.

And who is She, that shivering form,
  So lorn and yet so fair,
Like some spent angel, whom the storm
  Has forced to shelter there?
Faint, famished, worn, and ghastly pale,
Her dark locks waving in the gale,
  She, trembling, stands dismayed
Amid those fierce unfeeling men,
Like fawn that to the panther's den
  In evil hour has strayed.

Erewhile she blessed the pilgrim's cot
  With love's sequestered joy—
The Eve of his lone, exiled lot,
  The mother of his boy;
So like his sire in form and air,
When fondly in her wreathèd hair

He set the bridal rose ;
But now, nor home nor kin to bless,
The captive of the merciless,
    She treads the forest snows.

Still slept the ruffian band, nor stirred
    Amid those flickering gleams,
Save when, as broke some muttered word
    Upon their startled dreams,
Some dark hand seized the bow and shaft,
Or clutched the belt-knife's gory haft,
    As if the foe were nigh ;
But soon the larum thought passed o'er,
And sunk the lifted arm once more,
    And closed the glaring eye.

Softly as glides the mother where
    Her sleeping babe reclines,
So moved that lonely captive there,
    Beneath the moaning pines ;
As with despair's wild throb she knelt,
And from the slumbering sachem's belt
    His ruthless axe unloosed ;
Her husband's heart had stained the blade,
And to the haft, by one soft braid,
    Their first-born's scalp was noosed !

Then, as one armed with matchless might
    And heaven's vicegerent trust,

Sent with avenging sword to smite
    The guilty to the dust ;
She drove the crimson steel amain
Sheer to the sleeping murderer's brain
    With such destroying hand,
That when her fearful task was done,
Gory and gashed, there breathed not one
    Of that remorseless band.

O woman ! wont in sunny hour
    At thy own shade to start,
Yet when life's blackest tempests lower,
    High-soul'd and strong of heart ;
If once that mood is roused by shame,
Spurned love, wrecked hopes, or blighted name,
    Thy wronger needs beware ;
'Twere safer that his guilty path
Confront the whelp-robbed tigress' wrath,
    Than thy untold despair.

TO THE HILLS.

BROTHER bondman of the pen,
In this old midurban den,
Where, for weary months intent,
O'er these dismal tomes we've bent
Till our backs are well-nigh grown
To the rigidness of stone ;
In an atmosphere replete
With all odors but the sweet,
And such dissonance uncouth
That the deafest cit, forsooth,
Oft must muse, in vain surmise,
Why the ears, unlike the eyes,
Have not facile lids to close
'Twixt the hearing and its woes—
Brother Helot of the mart,
With the yearning, homesick heart
For green Berkshire, let's away
To the hills one blessed day,
Though the sore bonds sorer strain
When they have us fast again !

Ah, just think what careless glee
Waits our rural vagrancy,
When the truant feet once more
Kiss the dear old paths of yore !
Think of those white-clovered leas,
Murmurous with myriad bees,
Where we've mused in doubt profound,
Which were sweeter, scent or sound ?
Think of arbors draped with vines,
Near the lake's æolian pines,
In whose dim aisles even boys
Feel the impertinence of noise,
And steal, tiptoe, as in fear
Of some mystic presence near.
Think of sauntering once more
By the river's willowy shore,
To the spot where Naiad hands
Broad have scooped the russet sands,
For a laver brimmed with lymph
Meet for daintiest water Nymph
That e'er plashed the crystal flood
'Neath the white-armed buttonwood !
Doffing there our city gear,
Starch and gravity austere,
We'll show urchins thereaway,
What *our* fellows meant by " play "—
Meant by power of lung and tongue,
When we ancient lads were young.
Then, with freshened step and mien,
Ho ! for Ice Glen's weird ravine,

Where the mountain, wrenched apart,
Scarcely hides his mighty heart.
There, in bastions jagged and gray,
Winter holds the sun at bay ;
And in Arctic panoply,
Mocks all Summer's archery.
How we'll take the Oread's eyes
With a marvelous surprise,
As, in snowball range point-blank,
Each upon his guarded bank
Plies projectiles to and fro,
Till his cheeks are all aglow,
And his pelted garb is seen
White as miller's gabardine !

Brother bondman of the pen,
In this Babel-shaming den,
Let us steal ourselves away
To the hills one glorious day,
Though the gyves should sorer strain
When they have us fast again !

THE WONDER THAT MIGHT HAVE BEEN.

RUCE of Kinnaird could scarce repress the smile
   That twitched the bearded ambush of his mouth,
When, in his quest of the mysterious Nile,
   Amid the perilous wilds of the swart South,
An old man told him, with a grave surprise,
   Which made his childlike wonder almost grand,
How, in his youth, there fell from out the skies
   A feathery whiteness over all their land—
A strange, soft, spotless something, pure as light,
   For which their questioned language had no name ;
That shone and sparkled for a day and night,
   Then vanished all as weirdly as·it came ;
Leaving no vestige, gleam, or hue, or scent,
   On the round hills or in the purple air,
To certify their mute bewilderment
   That such a presence had indeed been there.

Yet, lady, who that sees, as here revealed,
  The constellated glories of the *Snow*,
From human vision hopelessly concealed
  Till art their hidden splendor deigns to show,
Can doubt if, when his native banks and braes
  The bronzed and weary Northman trod once
     more,
Your fairy lens had shown his dazzled gaze
  The whole broad landscape blazoned o'er and
     o'er
With crystal *Stars*—ay, who can doubt that he,
  Who at the simple Abyssinian smiled,
Would, at the sight of this strange galaxy,
  Himself have wondered like a little child!

CRADLE COVERLET.

INSCRIPTION :—FOR A CRADLE COVERLET OF BRILLIANT COLORS, EMBROIDERED BY A VENERABLE LADY FOR A FAIR IN AID OF THE SANITARY COMMISSION.

BOWED by the weight of fourscore years,
   And blinded by her widow's tears,
The daughter of a patriot sire
This earnest sends of fond desire
Her loving-kindness to attest
For brothers, stretched in sore unrest
Along the battle's crimson path
When the wild storm has spent its wrath.
She has done what she could—how few
Have better done, may better do,
As viewed by Him in whose clear sight
The offering of the widow's mite
Appeared more precious, being hers,
Than gifts of grandest almoners.

And Pity asks, with pleading tone :
Who'll make the hallowed prize his own ?

For the dear sake of those who pine
With bitter wounds, that thou and thine,
Walled by *their* breasts, might never feel
The fierce edge of the traitors' steel.

O wedded pair ! whose cradled love
Charms like a presence from above,
What brighter smiles your eyes shall trace
Upon the slumbering cherub's face
If, when the angels gather near
To whisper in his dreaming ear
The dear Christ's tender benison,
They mark the sinless little one
Invested in these tissued dyes
Lent from their own resplendent skies !

THE FALCON AND DOVE.

"TELL me, friend, the secret meaning
    Of this sculptured riddle, pray ; "
Quoth I to a sexton leaning
    On a tomb at shut of day.

Open, high embossed, was lying
    Heaven's blest Book of hope and love ;
And a marble falcon flying
    As in terror from a dove.

" Sir," replied the sexton hoary,
    Courteously as friend to friend,
" 'Tis a strange and mournful story,
    Weird and wondrous to the end.

" Where yon dome-like hill upswelling,
    Proudly lifts its silvan crown,
Lowers an outlaw's haunted dwelling,
    Shunned alike by thorp and town.

" Until passion's stress was over,
    And his sated soul craved ease,
He had been a desperate rover,
    Coursing all the round world's seas.

" Wealth he brought at his returning,
    Gold and gems in rare excess ;
But with whom and whence the earning,
    Few so dull as not to guess.

" Swart, and scarred, and grim of bearing,
    Dealt he, flash-like, oath or sneer—
Every word and look declaring
    Traits that mark the buccaneer.

" And there came a gentle creature
    To this mountain vale with him ;
Grief in every pallid feature,
    Pain in every feeble limb.

" Son he seemed, though faint the semblance
    To that dark and sullen man ;
Vague as Ariel's resemblance
    To the earth-born Caliban.

" Ne'er at parting, nor at meeting
    After weary task well done,
Fond farewell or kindly greeting
    Passed from scowling sire to son :

" Ne'er with keenest aggravation,
    In the lull of stormy ire,
Words of soft expostulation
    Passed from patient son to sire :

" As the wife had borne, while living,
    All his insults, mute and mild ;
So, all bearing, all forgiving,
    Suffered on the silent child.

" Wherefore should a sire be wreaking
    Outrage on an orphan son ?
Why, at every moment, seeking
    Anguish for his only one ?

' Serpent tongues had stung his bosom
    With the rankling lie malign,—
' What thou deem'st thy being's blossom,
    Is no real germ of thine ! '

" Then did Hope's enchanted palace
    Fall in ruins, wall on wall ;
Then was love's paternal chalice
    Brimmed with hate's envenomed gall ;

" And how oft, with aim abhorrent,
    Called he, now, to hunt the stag !
Leading o'er the swirling torrent,
    And along the dizzy crag ;

" To his weary victim shouting,
    When he faltered mid the snares :
'Coward !   Fear grows bold by flouting—
    Danger strengthens whom it spares !'

" But a form, unseen, was near him
    Ever on his perilled way,
O'er the dreadful pass to cheer him,
    On the giddy steep to stay.

" Oft in dreams it rose before him,
    Visibly, a snow-white Dove ;
And through swooping Falcons bore him
    To a land of peace and love.

" Foiled in all his fiendish scheming,
    Shrieked the sire with knitted brow
Wild as tortured guilt in dreaming :
    ' Prince of Darkness, aid me now !

" ' Take my broad fields black with cattle !
    Take my glittering hoards diverse—
All I've wrung from toil and battle—
    Rid me of this living curse ! '

" Lo, a flash and crash of thunder
    Whelm the bitter words apace ;
And a Shape of startling wonder
    Glooms before him, face to face.

"" 'Lost,' it scowled, 'is all such suasion !—
 Gold nor gems my power control—
These are mortals' bright temptation ;
 Mine, a brighter lure, the soul :

" ' Not thy soul, poor wretch, that pratest
 Of thy herded lands and pelf,
But the soul of him thou hatest—
 Thine is coming of itself !

" ' Where thy new-sown fields are greening,
 Send him forth at blush of day,
Charged, with threats of mortal meaning,
 Keep the wasting fowls at bay ! '

" ' Be it so,' the father muttered ;
 And, ere echo's nimble tone
Half the fiat had reuttered,
 Pale and grim he stood alone.

" Forth upon his fated mission
 Fared the friendless child forlorn,
Menaced with assured perdition,
 If he failed to ward the corn.

" Vain, alas, was his endeavor
 To obey the dire behest ;
For the winged marauders never
 Left him briefest space for rest !

" When he chased them from the valley,
    Swarmed they on the upland grain ;
Soon, when frighted thence, to rally
    In the vale's green lap again.

" Still, with patient zeal, unshaken
    He pursued his endless round,
Till at last of strength forsaken,
    Dropped he, swooning, to the ground.

" Lo, a strange form now beside him,
    And a white dove hovering near !
This, with yearning anguish eyed him,
    That, with ill-dissembled leer.

" Then with unabashed assertion,
    False as foul, the glozer said :
' Long I've marked thy vain exertion,
    And am come to bring thee aid.

" ' But as meed of faithful merit,
    When thy life's last moment dies,
Let me, for my own, inherit
    That which o'er the threshold flies ! '

" Sighed the youth : ' Kind sir, that taskest
    Time and strength to succor me ;
Though I wist not what thou askest,
    Be it thine whate'er it be ! '

" Sudden as an aspen's tremblance,
    Changed the Tempter form and face,
And a coal-black Falcon's semblance
    Dusked the sunlight in his place.

" Prince of air and all its minions,
    As of demon realms below,
Up he shot on whirring pinions,
    Swift as arrow from the bow.

" On he swept with fiery keenness,
    Now in tangent, now in whirl ;
Till o'er all the sprouting greenness
    Hovered throstle, crow nor merle.

" Then young Eve with rosy features,
    Bade the child no longer stay ;
And her fire-flies' fairy meteors
    Homeward lit his lonely way.

" ' Laggard ! ' cried the execrator,
    ' Why so late returned, I ask—
Have you truant played or traitor ?
    Skulked, or shirked your bidden task ? '

" ' No, my father ; watched I truly ;
    Watched and strove to guard the grain ;
But thy quest to answer duly,
    All my strivings were in vain,

"' Till a stranger kind befriending,
  Sought me at the noon of day,
And on raven wings ascending,
  Chased the hungry hordes away.'

"' Imp, with demon malice gifted,
  Take a tithe of thy unworth ! '
And the tyrant's arm uplifted
  Smote the guiltless to the earth.

" Like the bloodroot's snowy blossom
  Dabbled in its crimson flood,
Lo, the pallid brow and bosom
  Weltering in their own warm blood !

" On the morrow, lone and dying,
  Gazed the child with wondering fear,
On a pall and coffin lying
  At his bedside on a bier.

" Glaring eyes, the while, were keeping
  Watch within the open door,
And a fiend-like shadow sleeping
  Grimly on the sunny floor.

" Suddenly the watcher started,
  Shape and shadow fled amain,
As the White Dove weirdly darted
  Inward through the lifted pane.

" Round she flitted, moaning ever :
   ' Who of earth can sum thy loss,
If, when soul from body sever,
   Thine yon fatal threshold cross ? '

" *Now* his promise to the stranger,
   When he paltered at his side,
Woke the sufferer to the danger
   By these awful words implied ;

' And he cried with wild endearment :
   ' Hear me ! save me, sexton ! hear !
Fold me in my ready cerement,
   Lay me on my waiting bier !

' ' O'er the dreadful threshold bear me
   Forth beneath the blessed sky ;
Let not—oh, for mercy, spare me !
   Life and soul together die ! '

" Cried the ruffian murderer : ' Never !
   Hush thy mongrel, maundering breath !
May thy life and soul forever
   Perish utterly in death ! '

" Backward on his couch astounded,
   Fell the child in mortal fear ;
As if breaking heart-strings sounded
   Knell-like in his dying ear.

" Here my waiting pages entered ;
    And, despite threats, curses wild,
All our fondest cares we centered
    On the friendless, hopeless child.

" Tenderly we raised and laid him
    In his coffin on the bier,
Tenderly we thence conveyed him
    To the green lawn smiling near.

" There, as softer grew his breathing,
    Faintly dawned a hectic smile,
O'er the woful pallor wreathing
    Flush of inward peace the while.

" Then before his placid vision,
    Oped we clear the Book of Truth,
Where the Saviour's sweet decision
    Spake these words of tenderest ruth ;

" Saying : ' Suffer, unforbidden,
    Little ones to come to me ;
For in such, howe'er ye've chidden,
    Earth finds heaven's best simile.'

" Sudden now the light was parted
    By a shadow from above,
As the coal-black Falcon darted,
    Bolt-like, at the watchful Dove ;

" While, his shrouded form half raising,
    Like the widow's son of Nain,
  Sat the child, intently gazing
    On the eerie, eager twain.

" Now, aloft, they glanced and grappled,
    Now beneath the bier they met,
  Till the lawn around was dappled
    With their plumes of white and jet.

" Twice the worsted Dove was routed,
    Twice her fiendish foe she fled ;
  And the gloating ruffian shouted :
    ' Bravely, Falcon, hast thou sped ! '

"Braver yet is love's endurance—
    Love in faith's proof armor braced ;
  I replied, with fond assurance :
    ' Lo, the chaser now the chased ! '

" Swift through cloudland's blue dominion
    Fled the Falcon, round and round,
  Till the white Dove's swooping pinion
    Dashed him, cowering, to the ground.

" Down he vanished, as asunder
    Gloomed the ebon jaws of night ;
  And a deafening shout of thunder
    Shook the mountains at the right ;

" Whence a hollow voice came booming :
  ' Let the brat escape my lure ;
Since the sire awaits my dooming,
  Hither following, soon and sure ! '

" As we homeward thence were wending,
  In the calm bright skies above,
Saw we, side by side ascending,
  Dovelet white and snow-white Dove !

IN MEMORIAM.

I

N my young days a traveled stranger chanced
    To visit Berkshire, in his earnest quest
Of that arcadian heritage, which Hope,
With rosy finger pointing, tells each heart
Awaits it surely in the near beyond !
The fairest scenes whereon the morning smiles
With lingering gaze in many an orient land,
Had set their soft enchantments to his eye,
And whispered, " Seek no farther : " yet he passed
Still onward, till his feet at last were stayed
Within the magic circle of these hills.
Here was the Eden he had sought so long !
Here had his dream come true, and never more
Could fancy shake his faith, that all the vales
Of the wide world could boast no peer to this !
And here, like one imparadised, his life,
Exempt from idle longings and replete
With daily satisfactions, thenceforth lapsed
As gently as a placid stream that steals
O'er smoothest sands to its appointed bourne.

138

If such the local spell on sense and soul
Of this grave stranger, that he gave himself
A willing captive to these alien scenes,
And here would live, here die ; impassive, deaf
To all the pleadings, all the memories
That woo the wanderer to his native land ;
Were it not strange that they, whose eyes had gazed
From childhood on these charms of hill and vale,
Could ever leave them to return no more ?
Yet, to my thought, your heroes' absence seems
Less strange than would their presence here to-day;
Had they not heard, in duty's still small voice,
The voice of God and country, and at once
Wrenched loose their hearts from every dearest tie,
And marched right onward, even unto death ?
How could they falter when, that April morn,
The South wind whispered : " *War* is in the land !
I heard the thunder of his iron tramp ;
Saw the keen flash of his relentless steel
Affright the white-winged Peace from out her palms ;
And fled his frenzied presence, as he strode,
Dark frowning, Northward, and with lips ablaze
Fulmined his fierce anathemas on all.
Forewarned, confront him far off, ere he fall
Fullswing, resistless, on yourselves and yours ! "

Then, as the rattling larum of the drum
Rolled through these startled vales, uprose the
    might

Of Berkshire's martial manhood, and went forth
With stern face set as flint against the foe;
Despite the clinging of impassioned arms,
The pressure and the pleading of pale lips,
Whose farewells seemed the knell of Hope herself.

And ah! too truly, as the vacant seat
By hearth and board of lonely cottages
And social village mansions, sadly tells!
As tells more sadly still, the unheaved turf
Whence springs yon sacred column—turf forlorn,
That while its verdure wraps earth's common
    sands,
It may not fold your martyrs' precious dust.
No eye but that which marks the sparrow's fall,
Saw theirs, perchance, or ever shall discern
The places hallowed by their martial dust.
On lonely picket-guard beneath the stars,
Or in the starless watch of leaguered camps
Impalled in double gloom of night and storm,
They fell unseen; or in the battle-cloud
That dusks the blazing splendor of the noon,
Passed from their comrades' sight, as to and fro,
Whelming or whelmed, the swaying legions surged;
Or, fate's worst fate, were swept to nameless
    graves
From wards whose balms were blasphemies, whose
    shrift,
Curses gnashed fiercely into dying ears;

Or tumbreled forth from fiendish prison hells,
Gaunt, hunger-bitten skeletons, where Death,
In all his horrors, less abhorrent seemed,
Than had the ghastly life that perished there.

Ah, friends ! it were a mournful joy indeed,
Had fate but granted to your yearning hearts
The dear, disjewelled caskets, though no more
To beam with light unknown to sun or star.
How fondly had ye welcomed even these !
How tenderly consigned them to the rest
Of yon still chambers of the funeral sands ;
And felt their gloom illumined with the hope
That *there* your relics would be laid with theirs
For earliest recognition, face to face—
Face to face smiling with immortal smiles !

But though ye know not where the loved ones
        sleep,
On dreary downs or sunny inland glades,
By marge of lone lagoon or mountain stream,
Or in the dusk of ever-moaning pines ;
Know that, wher'er it be, their rest is sweet ;
Their couch assured of the great Mother's care.
Though there no human eye e'er drop a tear ;
No hand bring flowers or germ of future flowers ;
She, at whose all-sustaining breast were nursed
These Abels, murdered by fraternal hate
At duty's very altar, shall keep green,

With tempered largess of her dews and rains,
The turf that shelters their uncoffined dust ;
Or, when the year's disheveled tresses lie
Unsightly there, shroud all in spotless snows !

So, while to these maternal ministries
Sadly we leave the unreturning brave
Where the red battle left them stark and cold ;
Be ours the solace that they nobly died,
As ours the sacred duty to make sure
Their martyrdom shall not have been in vain !

BRIDEGROOM TO BRIDE.

EMBARKED at last, dear trustful wife,
   Before us, lo ! the voyage of life,
With all the hopes, and doubts, and fears,
That hover round our pilgrim years !
Yet, cheered with happy auspices
And fondest " Benedicites,"
Let us serenely, side by side,
Confront the dim and undescried.

O Sea ! that spread'st so smoothly now
Thy azure fields before our prow,
We know how soon the storm may chase
The shimmering dimples from thy face,
And even 'mid thy sunniest isles,
Supplant with frowns thy wonted smiles.
Yet, knowing this, we will not fear
Or storm or peril, far or near ;
Sure in our faith, oh, faithless sea,
That howsoe'er our bark may be
Tossed by thy waves' tempestuous will,
They must obey *His* " Peace, be still ! "

HARD-HANDS' PETITION.

THE chance to toil is all we ask ;
  O brothers, only this !
No matter what or where the task,
  It will not come amiss.

The lesser load or lighter strain,
  We stand not to discuss—
The task may go against the grain,
  And yet be dear to us.

Ungloved, the roughest thole we grasp,
  Nor burr, nor prickle heed ;
The nettle in our horny clasp
  Is but a silken weed.

We rather *earn* the crust we're fed,
  In fens or squalid slums ;
Than idle break the beggar's bread,
  Or twirl the pauper's thumbs.

Then grant the earnest toil we ask,
  Nor long the boon defer—
Who gives the poor an honest task,
  Is God's best almoner !

NEVER FEAR!

IN the journey of life never falter nor fear,
    Though danger may threaten an ambush of
        woes ;
If plainly the pathway of duty appear,
    Right on ! though it lead through a forest of
        foes.

The clouds that loom up in the distance so cold,
    Are blessings there falling in silvery showers ;
And the vales far away, now so drear to behold,
    Will change, as you near them, to vistas of flowers.

Yet should welkin and landscape but deepen the
        gloom
    They wore at the first, as the distant you win,—
Even then, friend, shall Hope, like the firefly, illume
    The gloom of the outward with beams from within.

And ponder not solely of Self as you go,
    For thousands, your brothers, move on by your
        side ;

Have a smile for their gladness, a sigh for their woe,
  A shame in their weakness, a pride in their pride.

Lend a hand to the feeble that totters to fall ;
  Speak cheer to the weary, o'erburdened with
      care ;
From youth's eager lip snatch the chalice of gall ;
  From beauty's charmed footfall, the myrtle-
      wreathed snare.

Let us strive, though of dust unto dust to return,
  As the flower to the sod whence it sprang to the
      day,
That all yet to traverse life's desert, may learn
  Our course by the roses we left on the way.

Though rugged the pathway and darkened the
      goal,
  With hope for the future and conscience the
      past,
Never fear, never doubt in the depths of the soul,
  That, spite of fate, all will be well at the last !

TO A FUNERAL WREATH.

OH, snow-white Wreath ! that graced but
      now
  Our dear Lucinda's shrouded rest
Not fairer than her marble brow,
  Nor purer than her stainless breast—
Would that thy flowers, so sacred made
  By that chaste shrine whereon they lay,
In holier beauty thus arrayed,
  Might never feel nor fear decay !

But, no, alas ! though tears like rain
  Upon thy blossomed circlet fall,
Love's fondest tribute were in vain
  To stay the blight that steals on all !
Admonished by that mortal shrine,
  How could we for a moment trust
That happier fate might yet be thine,
  Than hers—our dearest's—DUST TO DUST !

Nay, were the magic virtue ours,
  Oh, snow-white Wreath, so freshly blown !

To change thy frail memorial flowers
    To kindred forms of Parian stone ;
Amid our world of cypress glooms,
    Where life strives vainly with decay ;
Alas, even these marmoreal blooms,
    With crumbling years must pass away !

But thanks, dear friends, that when her feet
    Crossed the Dark Stream that waits for ours,
The dear one left our memories sweet
    With love's imperishable flowers—
Flowers of a soul whose happiness
    Consummate bloomed in grateful eyes ;
Whose constant thought was how to bless,
    Whate'er the stern self-sacrifice !

CENTRAL PARK.

OF all the gracious deities
    Ascribed of old to land or sea,
The god of Metes and Boundaries
    Henceforth shall be extolled by me !
For him I'll choose the fondest name
    The Muse in happiest mood can frame ;
And round it wreathe, in grateful lays,
    Her choicest flowers of love and praise.

For when the Commerce of the West,
    Her Empire mart majestic piled,
Nor recked how soon she thence might wrest
    The last green rood where Nature smiled ;
Lord Terminus, at once obeyed,
    The spoiler's march thus sternly stayed :
" Behold thy utmost bounds at last—
    Thus far, no farther, shalt thou blast !

" On all sides *round* this sacred pale,
    Be thine to ravage as of yore—
To lop the hill, to whelm the vale,
    And stifle all, from shore to shore,

With stately halls where anxious pride
    But *dreams* the peace to pomp denied ;
Or slums, whose horrors well may crave,
    For blest surcease, the pauper's grave !

" But all *within* this ample bound,
    This central sweep of lawn and lea,
Henceforth is consecrated ground
    Till earth herself shall cease to be.
No blast shall rend its living rock ;
    No rumbling wain its echoes shock ;
Nor sound of hammer, trowel, plane,
    Its silvan sanctities profane !

" Let no vain schemer dare deface
    Creation's master-touches here,
But Nature's every gift and grace
    In all their virgin charms appear ;
Save where congenial taste may serve
    To teach the stream a lovelier curve,
Or path a happier course to choose
    Where beauty veils still fairer views.

" No cruel act, no ribald speech,
    These peaceful shades shall e'er attest—
Within the schoolboy's easy reach
    The bird shall build and brood her nest ;
Nor shall the fawn to covert fly,
    When merriest groups go laughing by ;

But fearless in the wayside grass,
  Behold the jocund wonder pass.

"The turf shall teem with fairest flowers,
  E'er brought by guardians from the skies
To cheer their sublunary hours
  With bloom and breath of paradise ;
While murmuring streams and tuneful birds,
  And soft winds sweet with lovers' words,
And music's, sculpture's charms unite
  To thrill all bosoms with delight.

"What various forms of urban life
  Of every age, and sex, and sphere,
Shall daily steal from toil and strife,
  To find lost Eden's blessings here ;
To breathe large breath of balmy air ;
  Meet health and beauty everywhere ;
And feel a tingling rapture dart,
  In every pulse of Nature's heart !

"The noblest feast to mortals known,
  Is spread not for the palate's slaves—
'Man shall not live by bread alone ; '
  His soul diviner nurture craves ;
And here, in these serene retreats,
  It shall not lack abundant sweets
In every sight, and scent, and sound—
  Pure manna mantling all around ! "

TO A MINIATURE.

THE pictured face still wears the charm
   Her real presence used to wear,
When, circled by my loyal arm,
   She let me gaze enchanted there.

But since no more with dimpled wiles,
   She deigns my fondness to betray ;
Why cherish these unchanging smiles,
   Whose fickle types have passed away ?

A dearer arm now circles her ;
   Her beauty wiles a dearer heart—
Ah ! lost love's vain remembrancer !
   'Tis time for thee and me to part.

Go, then ! nor shall resentment find
   A harsher wish to send with thee,
Than that thy presence may remind
   How fondly once she smiled on me !

TO MEMORY DEAR.

THERE'S not a common pebble that hath been
For long a daily presence in our sight,
But memory values, when no longer seen,
As it had been a very chrysolite.

No little cherished flower of plainest dyes
Eludes our wonted smile and disappears,
Whose absence is not marked with wistful sighs,
Or, haply, even with the dew of tears.

But O the void of a beloved *face*,
That dearer grew with every passing hour,
For some new aspect of angelic grace,
Some sweeter bloom of love's incarnate flower !

TO ELIZABETH ON HER SECOND BIRTH-DAY.

OPENING bud of vernal life,
   Watched with smiles and tears !
Changing with the fitful strife
  Of love's hopes and fears—
Hopes that, with enchanting eyes,
Whisper of elysian skies,
And a sunny path, which lies
  Through a world of bloom ;
Fears that frown in hope's despite,
Muttering wild of storm and night,
And the swift untimely blight
  Of an early tomb !

Hope still speaks thy weal to Fear,
  Fear to Hope thy woe ;
Which will prove the wiser seer,
  Time alone can show :
I have learned that both may be
Prophets false of destiny,

Seeing what no ken can see
  In life's forward sky ;
But, as onward still we grope,
Let us fondly trust that Hope
Hath thy fate's dim horoscope
  Read with truer eye.

Yet in such a changing scene,
  Though thy lot be bright,
Clouds shall frequent pass, I ween,
  O'er thy spirit's light :
Maiden prime will bring its snares ;
Riper years their matron cares ;
Time at broadcast scatters tares
  Where he sows the flowers ;
And in spite of our endeavor
Loathed from lovely to dissever,
Side by side they twine, and ever
  Mingled crop is ours.

Beauty like a glory lies
  O'er thy being now,
Mirrored in thy glad blue eyes,
  And thy cherub brow,
Wreathed with many a glossy tress
Of such amber loveliness
As no poet can express,
  Paint he e'er so well ;
And the budding lip, that shows

Less of ruby than of rose,
And the dimpled cheek, which glows
  Like the rose-steeped shell.

Nursling of a rugged clime,
  These are now thy dower;
But o'er these the despot Time
  Hath a demon's power;
Speed can never foil his flight,
Darkness muffle from his sight,
Strength nor beauty stay his might,
  Though an angel plead;
Nature's self is but his thrall—
Oak and adamantine wall
At his ruthless summons fall
  Like a smitten reed.

Yet to wisdom's clearer sight,
  Murmur as we may,
Seems it vain to mourn the blight
  Of the flowers of clay;
Frailer and less fair than those
Which their tender charms disclose
By the marge of lingering snows,
  In some sunny vale;
Ere the earliest warblers bring
Tidings of the loitering Spring,
And while Winter's icy wing
  Shivers on the gale.

Therefore, fairest, do not trust
  To so vain a stay ;
Beauty's but a nicer bust
  Of earth's common clay ;
Born to no diviner mood,
Finer nerve or richer blood,
Than her favored sisterhood,
  Humbler gifted, are ;
Hour by hour her graces fly ;
Fast her cherished roses die ;
And the glory of her eye
  Setteth like a star !

But thy being's nobler **part,**
  Inly throned to reign
O'er the many-passioned heart
  And the restless brain—
Give to *that* o'ermastering power,
When the Will would snatch the flower
From temptation's upas bower,
  Though the asp be seen
Coiled within its charmèd dyes—
And, when earth in chaos lies,
Thou above the wreck shalt rise,
  Scathless and serene !

LINES

TO A DEAR FRIEND, WITH A PLAIN COPY OF
BRYANT'S POEMS.

THOUGH unadorned with pictured charms,
  With fretted gold, or flashing gem ;
I deem that friendship's thoughtful eye
  Will not my simple gift contemn.

For lacks it not intrinsic worth,
  Beyond the pride of wealth or art—
The beauties of a polished mind,
  The graces of a gentle heart :

One that, like Numa, oft has borne
  From haunted fount and voiceless glen,
The wisdom of a wiser lore
  Than marks the babbling schools of men :

One who hath drawn from passing bird,
  From falling leaf, and drooping flower,
Thoughts that shall light the memory's shrine,
  Till life's remotest hour :

One whose chaste pen ne'er traced a line
   To virtue false, to license dear ;
Which manly pride might blush to read,
   Or maiden purity to hear.

LINES

ON REVISITING BERKSHIRE LATE IN AUTUMN.

HOW slow the moons have waxed and waned,
    How dim their alien beams to me,
Since, fast in urban durance chained,
    Dear Mountainland, I've pined for thee !

When last, beneath these native skies,
    I gazed on hills and vales so dear,
The charm of Eden's vernal dyes
    Seemed mirrored in the landscape here.

The clover's breath embalmed the breeze,
    That danced from sunny knoll to knoll,
Repaying with the hum of bees
    The shades where sang the oriole.

But now, alas ! how changed the scene !
    No warbling woods, no murmuring blooms,
No groves with rustling arras green,
    The pride of summer's silvan looms !

Yet dearer, in their silent woe,
  Are these brown wastes and wilds to me,
Than all the gorgeous pomp and show
  Of that great mart beside the sea.

For let me feel beneath my feet,
  O native soil ! thy quickening thrill ;
And I, too, like the famed athlete,
  Thence gain new strength to wrestle still—

Still sorely toil, that wealth may fling
  Fresh ingots on his swollen heap ;
Still cope with cares, whose ruthless sting
  Disturbs the very death of sleep ;

With little means and large desires
  Conflicting in the silent mind,
That oft, in happier mood, aspires
  Its own fond tasks and times to find,

And be what manly pride commands,
  Life's nobler mission to fulfil—
No passive tool in sordid hands
  To work its wielder's reckless will.

DEATH.

A LL ! thou rememberest all
  Earth's breathing forms of every
name and lot;
  And bear'st the sable pall
With equal hand to palace and to cot,
Where pines the monarch on his pampered throne,
Or cowers the outcast watched by want alone !

  Bravely the eagle's plume
Bestems the gale, and sunward lifts his form
  Above the flashing gloom,
And volleyed terrors of the rushing storm ;
Yet vain that soaring wing's exulting might
To pass the range of thy dark arrow's flight.

  Wide o'er the polar waste,
Where life shrinks back from Winter's ghastly
  towers ;
  Wide o'er the green zones graced
With all the glorious blazonry of flowers,—
Yea, o'er each span of ocean's dark domain,
Are spread the trophies of thy conquering reign.

Empires of old renown,
Like giant phantoms, all have passed away—
The Macedonian's crown,
The Cæsar's pomp, the Goth's avenging sway,
Awake no terrors now, whilst every knee
Still bows in trembling fealty to thee !

Afar the tempest flings
Its warning thunders on the startled gale,
And far the simoom's wings
Forecast the portent of its coming bale ;
But thou, O dread, inexorable foe !
Sendest no herald of thy mortal blow.

Where the glad wine is quaffed,
And dance and song the giddy banquet crown,
Thou bear'st thy ruthless shaft,
Assassin-like, to strike thy victim down ;
Perchance the maid betrothed, or blushing bride,
Or laurelled idol of a nation's pride.

While bending o'er his lyre,
In the deep hush of night's inspiring reign,
Flushed with celestial fire
The mortal minstrel wakes his deathless strain ;
Thy hand, relentless at the purposed ill,
Arrests life's silver chords, and all is still !

Where guilt with innocence,
And pomp with squalid misery jostling meets ;
Thou, robed in pestilence,

At noonday stalkest through the shuddering streets ;
Till all is hushed where crowds were wont to tread,
Save the lone hearseman's call, " Bring forth your
    dead ! "

Nor smites thy swifter dart,
O blinded archer of the random aim !
The sere and leprous heart,
For years and years the haunt of sin and shame ;
Nor his, whose mad ambition's ruthless flood
Dyes nations crimson in their noblest blood :

Thou mak'st th' insatiate grave
Thine earlier garner for the pride of earth ;
The wise, the just, the brave,
The fair, the loved,—yea all of proven worth,
Thou snatchest from affection's scanty store,
Nor to its yearning breast return'st them more !

Yet to the pure in heart,
Who through temptation's many-sirened sea,
By faith's revealèd chart
Have shaped their perilled course unfalteringly,
Thou, like a pilot, welcomely dost come,
To bring life's weary bark to its last haven home !

WAITING FOR MORNING AT PROFILE MOUNTAIN.

SCARCE other token than the low sweet chant
　　Of unseen birds announced the coming
　　　　dawn ;
As, all impatient of the lingering night,
To this weird lake I groped my eager way.
I know the mountain giants are encamped
About me, scarce a bowshot from my feet ;
While yet no intimation is vouchsafed
Of presences so wondrous and so near.
Patience, O longing eyes ! for soon this gloom
Shall be transfused with floods of silvery sheen
Poured from the golden chalice of the morn ;
And all this now invisible array,
Stand forth in clear apocalypse sublime.

　　At last, O joy ! at last, hope long deferred
Becomes fruition as the darkness melts,
The gray mists vanish, and the dismal void,
Anon, is one vast sea of crystal air !
Rapt, motionless, oblivious of self,

I gaze on these imperial Sovereignties
With all the wonder of a waking child,
Whose last sight was dear faces ; whose first, now,
Phantoms more strange than thrilled his wildest
    dreams.

But who art Thou, whose throned sublimity
O'erkings these Titan majesties, and takes
Captive the gazer's soul with nameless awe ?
Few are the stormy centuries that have swept
Athwart thy cliff-hewn brother of the Nile ;
And lo, a formless and disfeatured mass
Is all the sculptured marvel that remains
Of man's eidolon of Cyclopic man ;
Whilst over thy immortal lineaments,
O Memnon of the Mountains ! harmlessly,
As the cloud's shadow o'er the granite glides,
Millions of years have passed, and left thy face
Clear-cut and sharp against the azure sky !
Thy lifted brow fronts Eastward, whence arise
The Shining Ones whose coming, morn and eve,
These glens first read in thy illumined smiles.
Thence, too, arose upon thy wondering gaze,
That light, before whose glory suns and stars
Put off their splendor—that Promethean flame,
Brought by the Mayflower from the throne of
    God,
To smite the rayless darkness from a world

"LOOK NOT THOU UPON THE WINE
WHEN IT IS RED."

 SOFT sleep the hills in their sunny repose,
  In the Land of the South, where the vine
      fondest grows ;
And blithesome the hearts of the vintagers be
In the grape-purpled vales of the Isles of the Sea !

And fair is the wine when its splendor is poured
Where glass beams to glass round the festival board,
While the magic of music awakes in its power,
And wit gilds the fast-falling sands of the hour.

Yet lift not the Wine-cup, though pleasure may swim
Mid the bubbles that flash round its roseate brim ;
For dark in the depths of the vortex below,
Are the sirens that haunt the red maelstrom of woe.

They have lured the gay spirit of childhood astray,
While it dreamed not of wiles on its innocent way ;

And the soft cheek of Beauty they've paled in its
    bloom,
And quenched her bright eyes in the damps of the
    tomb.

They have torn the live wreath from the brow of
    the Brave,
And changed his proud heart to the heart of a
    slave ;
And e'en the fair fame of the pure and the just,
With the gray hairs of age, they have trampled in
    dust.

Then lift not the Wine-cup, though pleasure may
    swim
Mid the bubbles that flash round its roseate brim ;
For dark in the depths of the vortex below,
Are the sirens that haunt the red maelstrom of woe !

THE OPTIMIST.

PRITHEE, friend, why always sad,
   Whatsoe'er the case is ?
Why contend our " world is bad,"
   In all times and places ?

Know that he, who thus complains
   Of this wondrous Nature,
Contumeliously arraigns
   Its divine Creator.

He pronounced it " very good ";
   But *you*, bold decryer,
Have the monstrous hardihood
   To make God a liar !

Unto His unerring eye,
   Faultless the inspection ;
And the Morning Stars on high
   Hymned the clear perfection.

You, who scarce can see your hand,
  At arm's length diminished,
Swear that worlds were badly planned,
  Botched, and left half finished !

" *Ours*, at least, where pain and sin,
  Leech and priest defying,
Claim us ere life well begin,
  Leave us but in dying ! "

Yes, but may not wisdom deem
  That e'en these dread phases,
In the universal scheme
  Have their rightful places ?

He who saw the perfect whole
  While 'twas yet ideal,
Faulted not in sand or soul,
  When He made it real.

Think you that His wise intents
  By mere chance succeeded ?
That He fashioned instruments
  Never used nor needed ?

Pain and pleasure, good and ill,
  In themselves or actors,
All are workers of His will,
  All are benefactors.

Had there been no Lucifer
  'To the world's temptation,
'There had been no Crucifer
  For the great salvation.

Though our earth be but a speck
  On creation's border,
It could never suffer wreck
  Without worlds' disorder :

Orbs above it, orbs below,
  All concatenated,
Needs must feel a kindred throe,
  Were't annihilated.

Orb and atom—each is just
  What and where it should be ;
Otherwise the Cosmos must
  Fail of what it would be.

Even one so mean as I,
  Born for humblest kneeing,
Links still humbler with the high,
  In the chain of being.

Let us, then, submissive rest
  In our several station,
Sure that all is for the best,
  Throughout all creation !

OJOURNING lately at an hostelry
    Not many miles from Washington, D. C.,
I, who am dwarfed alike by stout and tall,
Could not but feel ridiculously small,
When, to the attic summons of my bell,
A dark Hyperion promptly answered, " Well ? "
A nobler presence, form of grander mold,
Of shapelier limb, or power more manifold,
My eyes had rarely lighted on till then,
In all their wide remark of model men.
" Well ? " he repeated, as my anxious sight
Surveyed the airy distance of the height
I needs must measure, should he, haply, please
To hurl me headlong (and he could with ease),
For ringing up, though unaware indeed,
So grand a server of a trivial need.
But soon recovering from my blank surprise,
And squarely meeting his unswerving eyes,
I said, as one preposterously brave :
" Are you, forsooth, a—pardon me—a *slave ?* "

"Slave !" he retorted with a bitter smile,
And nervous tapping of his breast the while,
" I bought of my own father, truth to say,
For a great price, this unpaternal clay ;
And, as I paid in full, *I* surely ought
To be the owner of the thing I bought ! "

LINES

AS o'er the crystal element
    The Queen of Eden careless bent,
She started back with frank surprise
At the sweet face that met her eyes ;
Yet looked again, and gazing on
The upward-gazing paragon,
She felt, perforce, as beauty will,
Her pure cheek flush, her bosom thrill,
To recognize her own fair face
In perfect reflex, grace for grace !

So when, at times, my gentle friend
O'er Shakspeare's magic page shall bend,—
Where Genius in its happiest mood
All loveliest traits of womanhood
Has mirrored in immortal lays,—
She, too, shall start with fond amaze,
To see the imaged counterpart
Of her own maiden mind and heart,
In Portia's, Juliet's sister mien,
And the white soul of Imogen.

CLERK-VESPERS IN WALL STREET.

TWELVE hours since morn I've toiled away,
　　Dear hours of blithesome boyhood, yet
As one who never dreamed of play,
　　Or dreamed but to forget.

I know not what the day has been
　　Abroad beneath the vernal skies,
I only know that here within
　　It seemed of sombre guise.

Perchance on circling hills the while,
　　And flowery slope and dimpled bay,
'The golden sunlight's softest smile
　　Has played the livelong day.

Yet what is Spring's glad light to him,
　　Or earth's fresh lap whereon it falls,
Whose heaven is yonder sky-light dim,
　　Whose scope, these dingy walls?

Here is my world, relieved by nought
   Of swarded green or vaulted blue ;
Here, day by day, must thews and thought
   The same dull task pursue.

Chained to the oar, like galley-boy,
   When youth would float with pleasure's tides,
I row against the stream of joy,
   And gaze the way it glides.

But thanks to thee, returning Eve,
   That smil'st with starry eyes so fair,
And bring'st the blest though brief reprieve
   From this dull round of care !

Hence ! figured tomes, whose soulless lore
   But treats of Mammon's loss or gain ;
I feel your shadows fall once more
   Alike from heart and brain.

Farewell ! till morn, the din and jar,
   The tumult of the bustling street,
The rumbling of the ponderous car,
   And tramp of eager feet.

The loveliest of suburban nooks,
   All green with rustling vine and bough,
And voices sweet, and fond, fond looks
   Await my coming now.

And, haply, o'er the moonlit dews,
  When sleep has hushed those voices sweet,
For trysting dear night's coyest muse
  Shall seek my green retreat ;

And, with some charm of measured thought,
  Again bid joy's reviving wings
Forget what cares to-day has brought,
  And what to-morrow brings.

IT IS WELL WITH THE CHILD.

SIMPLE pebble from the brook,
   That daily wins a passing look
By some quaint charm of form or hue,
We miss not from our wonted view,
Without a natural regret
To lose e'en such a humble pet.
More natural still the tender pain,
When ours the lot to look in vain
For *living* object, bird or flower,
Whose charm has solaced many an hour,
And made the very sick-room seem
The precinct of a dulcet dream.
But when inexorable Fate
Will make us most disconsolate,
She snatches from our yearning sight
Some nearer, dearer heart's delight—
Some spirit from the realms of day
Embodied in our mortal clay ;
Like thine, dear little friend, whose face
Beamed on us with such winning grace,

As made each glance, wherever met,
The sunniest and the sweetest yet !
And daily to our longing eyes
Its vanished smiles will fondly rise ;
And, nightly, blend their angel gleams
With memory's most hallowed dreams ;
Till, haply, in that happier clime
Beyond these brooding mists of time,
We meet the dear ones gone before,
Imparadised for evermore !

LINES

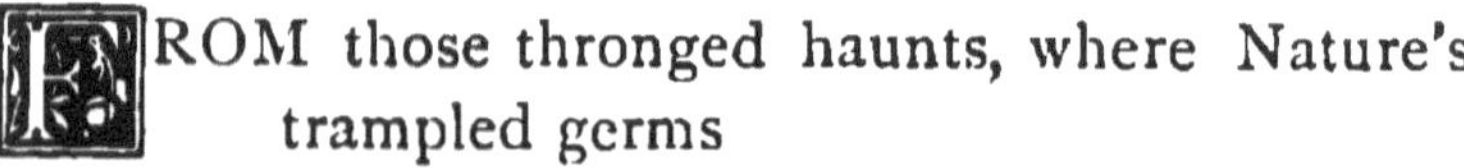

FROM those thronged haunts, where Nature's
    trampled germs
Ne'er feel the touch of Spring, nor wake to wear
Her green and perfumed garniture again,
Escap'd at last, like vassal disenthralled,
I stand upon thy silvan marge once more,
O fairest mirror! where the placid Morn
Surveys her blushing loveliness, or Eve
The wondrous glory of her starry train !
Yet bears the image gazing at me now,
Far other aspect than was wont to smile
On boyhood's bending vision ; though the boy
And he that sighs to mark the mournful change,
Are still the same. Sad change, indeed !—yet
    thanks,
Thanks, dear magician ! in whose faithful glass
I read that time may pale the flush of youth,
May blanch the raven locks, and earthward bend

The wan and wrinkled tablet of the brow ;
Yet leave the heart's first records uneffaced,
And all its Geyser-fountains bubbling still.
Therefore to thee and these associate scenes,
Whate'er this outward seeming, I have brought
The fresh, warm feelings, and the memories dear
Ye nursed within my breast in vernal years.
Despite the past, I *am* a boy again !
And soon from yon dim grotto as of yore,
A fairy bark shall leap into thy waves,
And fling its white folds bravely to the breeze
In gay defiance ; nor shall he whose hand
Directs its billowy fleetness, heave a sigh
For broader ocean or more witching isles
Than these my own dear native hills embrace.
And when the stormy spirit of the North
Has hushed thy liquid murmurs, and consigned
Thy dimpled beauty to a rigid waste,
The boy of two-score winters oft shall join
The hamlet's merry troop, careering wild
On steel-shod sandals o'er thy smooth expanse ;
While ring the echoing dells with louder mirth,
When sheer beneath our swiftly-gliding feet,
Thunders the sudden cleft from shore to shore .

And she who bends in childhood's strange delight
Above the pale sweet face soft mirrored there,
As if thy loveliest Naiad's sister eyes
Were smiling up in hers, shall haunt with me

Thy winding bays, green isles, and headlands bold,
And deem that Tempe in its vernal prime
Could boast no charms that were exotic here.
To her, erewhile in urban durance pent,
Earth's verdant lap, perfumed with floral hues,
And laced with silver streams, was all unknown ;
Nay, yonder Sun, bedimmed by sulphurous clouds,
And shorn of half his realms by Art's proud piles
Upheaved in gloomy grandeur to the sky,
Has never taught her wondering soul till now,
With what a godlike glory he comes forth
From morning's rosy portals, and at eve
Smiles from his golden chambers of the West.
The time has been when one poor sickly flower,
One dwarf'd shrub pining in the dim, damp court,
And one pet bird, unconscious as herself
Of bloomy lawns and many-minstrelled groves,
Were all she knew of Nature ; but henceforth
Her path shall wind through fields so pranked with
    flowers,
That oft her lifted foot shall seek in vain
For space whereon to light, nor harm the bee ;
Or steal through warbling wilds so arched with
    boughs,
And roofed with myriad leaves, the noon-day sun
Ne'er sees the moss on which their shadows sleep.
And ah ! should that young cheek's too lingering
    flush,
Like Autumn's hectic hues, presage decay,

Still hope is ours, that thou who sendest forth
Thy cooling mists upon the evening winds,
To bless with gentle showers or gentler dews
The lowliest herb that withers in the waste,
Hast yet a healing balm for this dear flower,
Snatched from the rough Zahara of the world
To bloom in thy glad presence, fairy lake,
And crown the glory of thy perfect charms.

THE PARTING BY THE SEA.

ONE more embrace, sweet one, the last
  For long, long months, perchance for years !
The loosed sail climbs the dizzy mast,
  The pilot at his helm appears ;
And hark ! the imperious *All ashore !*
Alas !—yet one—*one* last kiss more !

Now, though thou canst not hear the prayer
  We lingering breathe beside the sea :
Our wafted kisses still shall bear
  Sweet messages of love to thee,
As long as brimming eyes can trace
Thy form across the widening space.

O vernal winds ! whose fickleness
  The palm of change may justly claim,
For once your wanton mood repress,
  And, sobered to a steady aim,
Speed onward, with unwavering breath,
The bark that bears Elizabeth !

And when her pilgrimage is o'er,
  Her memory made a pictured shrine
For shapes and scenes which classic lore
  Has touched with splendor half divine ;
O faithful winds ! still fair abaft,
The loving to the loving waft !

THE LAST WATCH.

O-MORROW, Greenwood's turf must fold
  These dear remains from mortal sight—
Ah ! slowly let the sands be told,
  That bring the parting anguish, Night !

As o'er the shrouded form we bend,
  Our souls with fond illusions thrill—
Sweet dreams, that thou, departed friend,
  In this pale sleep art with us still.

But never more from such eclipse
  Shall morn those gentle eyes relume,
Nor ever more on those cold lips
  Shall wit its smiling throne resume !

Nor shall that voice, so soft and sweet,
  Again in silvery accents flow ;
Or that dear hand, delighted, meet
  Our own in friendship's heart-warm glow !

Yet, Charles ! till we, who watch and weep,
   In turn are gathered earth to earth ;
Our souls with vestal care shall keep
   Undimmed the record of thy worth.

How soon must Greenwood's turf enfold
   These dear remains from love's fond sight !
Ah ! slowly let the sands be told,
   That bring the parting anguish, Night !

LINES TO A DEAR YOUNG FRIEND.

AS men have watched the starry skies,
   To herald fate's decree;
So have I gazed in thy young eyes
   To learn thy destiny;
But in their azure depths of light
   No prophet-sign appears,
·To mark thy life for early blight,
   Or long and happy years.

Yet, let no fear of future ill
   Thy sunny smiles o'ercast!
Spring holds not back her budding sweets,
   For menaced blight or blast;
Nor deem it hard that change on change
   Betides our steps below;
Earth were too dear if all were joy,
   Too drear if all were woe.

Life's mingled chalice, then, dear friend,
   With calm acceptance greet;

Not mindless of its bitter drops,
   Nor thankless for its sweet ;
And trust, that though thy future path
   Through wastes forlorn may lie ;
The care that guards the desert bird,
   Will fount and food supply !

BROTHER TO BROTHERS.

ROM the four winds we are come,
    Brothers, to this gracious home,
Each at Alma Mater's knee
To be trained impartially
For the post his bent, not whim,
Plainly points as best for him
Where to strike for truth and right
With a a loyal champion's might.

Who shall say that ours is not,
Every way, a favored lot ?
While in yonder busy streets
Toil his weary tasks repeats,
Plying hammer, trowel, plane,
Urged by need, or greed of gain ;
Here we take our easeful seat
At some sage Gamaliel's feet,
While he turns the classic page,
And exalts the heritage
Left by genius graced to find
Richest ingots of the mind,

And to coin the precious store
For world-treasures evermore ;
Or he bids the Gnomes reveal
What their rayless realms conceal ;
Bids the Naiads rob the seas
Of their untold mysteries ;
Or the restless Sylphs declare
Their coy wonders of the air ;
Or Urania disclose
How the starry hosts arose,
And, in circling order bright,
Interchangeing day and night,
With their orreries sublime
Mete the cosmic march of time.

Brothers, wheresoe'er at last,
Fate our severed lives shall cast ;
In the pauses of the strife,
Which awaits all earnest life,
These quaternion years will seem
Like a brief Elysian dream,
Which, with many a fond refrain,
We shall dream and dream again !

When the knell of college-days
Tolls us to the parting ways,
(Nevermore, perchance, to meet !)
And our unreturning feet
Bear us far and farther from
This our dear fraternal home,

We shall see in Memory's glass,
All its varied past repass—
See these groves where we have strayed
As in Academus' shade,
Musing Science' endless themes,
Rapt with poets' vivid dreams;
See each grave Gamaliel's brow
Fondly anxious then as now;
And each comrade's face, the while,
Meet and greet us, smile for smile!

Brothers! near or far apart,
Let us so keep hand and heart
True to every duty's claim,
Pure from every soil of shame,
That no sighed "alas!" be heard
For one thoughtless deed or word,
When or where in Memory's glass,
We shall see our past repass!

INTRODUCTORY LINES FOR A FRIEND'S ALBUM.

EAR friends, these leaves so pure and white,
    Just as they are, can give delight
To eyes that have been blest to see
A charm in spotless purity.
Nor deem me vain, if *I* confess
To feel that charm's delighfulness
In these fair blanks, as now they are,
Without one fleck or speck to mar!

But what a deeper pleasure still,
In after years my heart shall thrill,
When, bending o'er these tablets dear,
I read what love has written here!
Even *now*, from out this stainless white,
Fond words steal clearly on my sight,
And sweetly whisper in my ear
Heart-greetings, tender and sincere.

But when these fancied words shall stand
Revealed, at last, by friendship's hand;

What crowning joy shall then be mine,
As, lingering o'er each gracious line,
My eyes in every sentence trace
The writer's very form and face ;
While breathes his voice, so near, so dear,
From all the precious souvenir !

THE TEMPTATION.

THE merchant prince had retired for the
day,
And clerk after clerk had dropt away,
Till at last remained but a single one
At his weary desk and his task undone,
As slowly the twilight's spectral gloom
Shut down on the lonely counting-room,
Whose ponderous safe's forgotten key
Seemed to whisper, " Lo, open Sesame !"
Then wierdly stole on the toiler's ear :
" Ho ! slave of the thriftless pen, look here !
Lo ! riches to win one a royal bride—
The coast is clear, and the world is wide ;
By the forelock seize opportunity,
Or grovel in life-long drudgery ! "
Then the safe key turned in the massy ward,
And the door swung ope of its own accord,
Disclosing a glamour of treasures untold,
Ingots and coffers compact of gold ;
And again there glozed in the young clerk's ear,
" The world is wide, and the coast is clear ;

Make free, and away o'er the trackless sea—
Wealth everywhere sails in brave company!"

But hark ! like the moan of passing-bell,
A low, stern voice on the silence fell :
" Make free, if thou wilt, and away o'er the sea—
But *these* are the comrades shall sail with thee :
Contempt for the honor that could not withhold
Its hand from the grasp of another's gold ;
Remorse for the lessons so lightly spurned,
From tenderest lips in thy childhood learned ;
Despair for the sinister bar of shame
Burnt into the shield of an honored name ;
Soul-yearnings for voices and faces that ne'er
Shall be heard but in dreams, but in dreams shall
        appear ;
And *Conscience*, commissioned to antedate
The tortures assigned to the afterstate ;
And *Terror*, the bloodhound that night and day
Hangs hard on the heels of its felon prey—
Let him fly to the shrine, let him cower in the gloom
Of the robber's cave or the eremite's tomb ;
Let him rove with the corsair, or flit with the
        bands
Whose barbs mock pursuit to the mid-desert
        sands ;
No refuge so distant, no gloom so intense,
But the bay of that bloodhound shall startle him
        thence,

And harrow and haunt him o'er waste and o'er
    wave,
To the outlaw's den or the suicide's grave ! "—·
Ah ! pause, ere thou set the black seal to thy fate
With the hand that makes free with such perilous
    freight ;
Nor launch thy young soul on life's treacherous seas,
For a haven forlorn, with such comrades as these !

NOTHING LOST.

ALL forms in this fair world of ours
   Are heirs alike of sure decay—
Alps, Andes, adamantine towers,
   Dissolving, perish day by day !
Yet valleys wax, as mountains wane
   Before the touch of fire or frost ;
Forms change, their elements remain,
   This gaining what the other lost.

The lucid drops in beauty's eye
   Were once the rainbow's softer flame ;
A few brief hours, and yonder sky
   Its sparkling jewels will reclaim,
To gleam in cloudland's sapphire hall,
   Snow-stars or gems of opal rain ;
Till earth the crystal waifs recall,
   To glow in beauty's orb again.

TO DASYA ELEGANS.

WHY were ye formed so graceful and so fair,
  To wave in dim recesses waste and lone ?
Why do your fronds such purple splendor wear,
  As never yet at Tyrian bridal shone ?

In deep seclusion, far from human sight,
  Where ocean valleys wind in glimmering glocm,
What eye is near to kindle with delight
  And grateful wonder, at your matchless bloom ?

Yet will I deem not ye were born in vain,
  Nor fancy yours an unregarded lot,—
No, lovely links in being's living chain,
  Wise ends ye serve, though man may guess them
    not !

For him, perchance your wafted virtue lends
  A balmier freshness to the ocean breeze ;
Perchance for him your purple beauty blends
  A softer azure with the sky's and sea's.

Nor will I doubt that in your native fields,
  Far from our dusty haunts of toil and care,
Your tinted grace a dear enchantment yields
  To eyes that watch your bright unfoldings there.

For 'tis my faith, that in the deepest night
  Of sparry grottoes, as in statued aisles,
No form of beauty there but gives delight,
  And smiles the lovelier for reflected smiles.

INVOCATION TO WINTER.

AS one, whose bosom's burdened with the charge
Of mournful tidings,lingers on the way
His errand leads him, falters at the gate,
And stops with fond misgiving by the door
Whence joy must vanish as he lifts its latch ;
So come thou, Winter ! messenger forlorn,
With slow and sad reluctance ; pausing oft,
And oft averting thy disastrous face
From scenes thy presence, like a sombre cloud,
Must disenchant of all their sunny smiles.
We are become so pampered with the beams
And balms of Summer, that thy very name
To us, as to the tropic relegate
Amid the shivering horrors of the North,
Is but the doleful synonym of pain.
Oh, regent of inexorable foes !
Leave us a little longer, we implore,
The soft beatitude of genial days,
The feel of Summer's scarce abated glow
In Autumn's languid pulses ! Leave us still

Sweet blandishment of winds, whose gentle breath
Seems but the tempered refluence of June's
Without her roses ! Leave us still, we pray,
The hum of bees in clovered aftermaths ;
And, dearer yet, the song of lingering birds,
Who would not heed the swallow's prescient call
To climes that never dream of one like thee !

The sky is full of many-featured days—
Days fierce and grim, days of celestial smiles,
Which cheer and cherish all the forms of life.
O scare not, frown not back with stormy ire,
Impatient, these serene benignities !
Let there still linger round the couch of pain
Soft benedictions of the sun and air !
Let Age creep forth, and in their genial warmth
Forget the frosts that numb his trembling limbs ;
And let the homeless child still find a hearth
In every stone that woos his naked feet
To share the blessing of its latent beams !
Thy crystal seal of silence set not yet
Upon the silvery lips of tinkling streams ;
Nor on the murmurous laughter of glad lakes
To shimmering dimples kissed by fairy winds ;
And oh, not yet, not *yet*, we pray, despoil
The silvan realm of its imperial robes
By Iris woven in her magic looms ;
But let our charmèd wonder still survey
The glorious vision, as the favored guests
That walk the tiring-chambers of a king !

TO THE JOSEPHS AND PHARAOHS OF THE WEST.

(TIME OF THE FLOUR RIOTS.)

OH, ye hard-handed, not hard-hearted yoemen,
   Whom bounteous Ceres crowns with plen-
      teousness ;
Pray do not prove your city-cousins' foemen,
   In this their bitter hour of sore distress !

While Autumn's latest leaves are round us falling,
   And first furs walk the gusty promenade ;
We hear the voice of Winter wildly calling
   His ruthless legions to their annual raid.

How shall our gaunt and half-starved ragamuffins,
   Whose very sight would melt the soul of Puck,
Encounter these remorseless Arctic ruffians
   With any decent show of manly pluck ?

The while your barns and bins are overflowing
   With all the treasures of the bounteous year ;

And your round cheeks and double chins are show-
    ing
  The hale and ruddy glow of generous cheer ;

Grim want with livid lips and ghastly pallor,
  Where Death himself might deeper horror learn,
And homelessness, and nakedness, and squalor,
  Confront our shrinking steps at every turn.

'Twould seem as if there'd been a league of nations,
  Wherein all tongues and tribes had taken part,
At once to kidnap all their poor relations,
  And foist the living mass on our doomed mart.

Outcasts Asiatic, Libyan, European,
  From all the round world's continental shores
To the remotest isles antipodean,
  Besiege from morn till night our hapless doors ;

And as they shrink before the grim December,
  Drowning his wild blasts with the cry for bread,
There's something more for pity to remember
  Than wealth's cold comfort, "Be ye clothed and
    fed !"

Then hold not Ceres in ignoble durance,
  That later ransom may enlarge reward ;
Shell out ! nor doubt the blessed Book's assur-
    ance :
  "Who helps the needy lendeth to the Lord !"

ONCE ON A TIME.

(HALLECK, RED-JACKET AND BOZZARIS.)

JUST below Niblo's, west southwest,
In a prosaic street at best,
I chanced upon a lodge so small,
So Liliputian in all,
That Argus, hundred-eyed albeit,
Might pass a hundred times, nor see it.
Agog to learn what manikin
Had shrined his household gods therein,
With step as light as tiptoe fairy's
I stole right in among the Lares.
There, in the cosiest of nooks,
Up to his very eyes in books,
Sat a lone wight, nor stout nor lean,
Nor old nor young, but just between,
Poring among the figured columns
Of those most unmelodious volumes,
Intently as if there and then
He conned the fate of gods and men.

Methought that brow so full and fair,
Was formed the poet's wreath to wear ;
And as those eyes of azure hue,
One moment lifted, met my view,
Gay worlds of starry thoughts appeared
In their blue depths serenely sphered.
Just then the voice of one unseen,
All redolent of Hippocrene,
Stole forth so sweetly on the air,
I felt the Muse indeed was there ;
And feel how much her words divine
Must lose, interpreted by mine.

" For shame," it said, " Fitz-Greene, for shame !
    To yield thee to inglorious thrall,
And leave the trophy of thy fame
    Without its crowning capital !

" The sculptor, bard, as well may trust
    To shape a form for glory's shrine,
If, ceasing with the breathing bust,
    He leave unwrought the brow divine.

" How oft the lavish Muse has grieved
    O'er hopes thy early years inspired ;
And sighed that he who much received,
    Forgot that much would be required.

" But not too late, if heeded yet,
    The voice that chides thy mute repose,

And bids thee pay at last the debt
  Thy genius to Parnassus owes.

" 'Tis not enough that pride may urge
  Thy claims to memory's grateful lore,
And boast, as rapt from Lethe's surge,
  The Suliote and the Tuscarore.

" Nay, bard, thy own land's mighty dead
  Deserve a nobler hymn from thee,
Than bravest of the brave that bled
  At Laspi or Thermopylæ.

" Remember, then, thy young renown,
  Thy country's dead, thy Muse's sigh ;
And bid thy vigorous manhood crown
  What youthful genius reared so high ! "

TO VIRGINIA.

MOTHER of Statesmen ! scorn to wreak
   Thy vengeance on a fallen foe ;
The more, for that he turns the unblenched cheek
  To meet the deadly blow.

Recall thy sons' heroic stand
  The tyrant's haughty rage to stem ;
Championed by him whose birthplace makes thy
    land
  Akin to Bethlehem.

Undo the helpless captive's chain
  From limbs already cramped with age ;
Let not his gray hairs shame, his thin blood stain,
  Thy history's noble page !

Bid him go forth and sin no more ;
  But give to prayer and penitence
The few, fleet moments haply yet in store,
  Ere *God* shall call him hence.

Though, glorying in his frenzied deed,
  He reck not how the blow may come ;
Crown not fanatic error with the meed
  Of saintly martyrdom !

THE ENCHANTRESS.

WITH pencil dipped in richest dyes
　　That flowery fields or sunset skies
E'er lavish on our wondering sight,
She touched the tablet's spotless white,
And lo, such forms of beauty start
To life, responsive to her art,
As only grace, with charms supreme,
The Eden of a poet's dream !
But vain were poet's happiest phrase,
In happiest mood for fondest praise,
To symbolize the witching spell
Of this divine art miracle.
Affrighted by the prying gaze
And tumult of these boisterous days,
'Tis said the Fairies and their Queen
Can no more, anywhere, be seen
Beneath the moon, in mead or dell,
Though all the world watch e'er so well.
Not so, Enchantress ! Fairy Land,
Restored by thy creative hand,
Smiles on us in these forms and hues,
As sweetly as on Shakespeare's muse

It smiled by Avon's haunted stream,
In that most sweet Midsummer Dream :
And were our failing sight less blurred
With unshed tears for hopes deferred,
It could not fail to recognize
A fairy form, and fairy eyes
Outpeeping from each covert screen
Of leaves, and flowers, and mosses green,
Depicted with such skill divine,
That Nature would not change a line.

TO NAPOLEON THE "GREAT", 1848.

L IKE the peal of distant thunder
  Booming through the sullen night ;
Like the earthquake's rumbling shudder
  Paling cities with affright,
Swells the roar of revolution
  Far o'er palaced hills and plains,
From the hearts of trampled millions
  Blindly bursting from their chains.

Oh, for one of lordly presence,
  One of genius all sublime,
On whose brow in light were written :
  WORTHY OF THE TASK AND TIME !
Gloriously to solve the problem
  With the sword of CHARLEMAGNE :
" What shall be the fate of Europe,
  Cossack or Republican ? "

Hark ! methinks the stifled murmur
  Of avenging wrath and shame,

Growing to articulate utterance,
  Syllables at last a name ;
One whilom that thrilled the tyrants
  With a more than mortal dread ;
One Valhalla's proudest welcomed,
  Mightiest of the warrior dead !

Victor in a hundred battles,
  In as many hostile lands,
'Twixt the Moskwa's frozen horrors
  And Syene's burning sands ;
From thy bannered mausoleum,
  Towering o'er the mournful Seine,
Wakened by the shout of nations,
  Burst upon the scene again !

Not in pomp of royal purple,
  Sceptre, crown, and oriflamme,
Such as erst thy triumph blazoned
  In resplendent Nôtre-Dame ;
But as when France first received thee,
  Lord of humbled Austria ;
Nobler in thy plain gray saga,
  And thy simple chapeau-bras.

When around thy surf-beat dungeon
  Wildly raved the midnight blast,
TÊTE D'ARMÉE sublimed the tumult
  As thy stormier spirit passed !

How sublimer were the echo
  Of thy dying words to-day,
Could the voice of mustering millions
  Hail thee FREEDOM'S Tête d'armée !

Wake, O wake, then, sworded sleeper,
  From thy bivouac of death !
Thou whose nostril's living ether
  Was the cannon's fiery breath :
Lo ! against the hosts of tyrants
  Freedom's host its phalanx knits—
Wake, and to the People's battle
  Bring the sun of Austerlitz !

Never yet in all their perils,
  All their agonies, till now,
Have they needed such a MENTOR,
  Such a present MARS as thou,
'Gainst their banded foes to lead them,
  With thy old prophetic trust,
Till the last of throned oppressors,
  Crushed and crownless, bite the dust.

Then, resumed thy martial cerements,
  Sleep the dreamless sleep again,
In thy bannered mausoleum,
  Towering o'er the joyous Seine ;
Hailed with grateful REQUIESCAT,
  Breathed from every peopled clime :
THIS TIME FAITHFUL TO HIS MISSION,
  WORTHY OF HIS TASK SUBLIME !

CENTENNIAL ECHOES.

VERSES READ AT THE CELEBRATION OF THE HUNDREDTH
ANNIVERSARY OF LEE, MASS., SEPTEMBER 13, 1877.

KIND friends, if idle fame has raised
    The pleasing expectation,
That rhymes of mine were like to lend
    One charm to this occasion ;
Pray do not blame the simple bard
    For his compliant ditty ;
But charge the disappointment all,
    To your insane Committee !

They feared no lack of racy "*prose*,"
    Both joyous and pathetic ;
But even *that* would please the more,
    If pranked with foil poetic ;
And, therefore, have I greatly dared
    To face your focal glances,
While my decrepit lyre intones
    A tale of rhythmic fancies :—

The scene was Nature's model vale,
  Where, after long reflection,
Like Zeuxis, she had grouped ana posed
  Each borrowed charm's perfection—
The fairest hills, the gayest meads,
  The clearest lakes and fountains—
And set the living picture in
  A frame of graceful mountains.

But sons of that first woful pair
  Who brought the curse of toiling,
Descried the wonder, and began
  Their round of Eden-spoiling ;
They felled the warbling groves,and gashed
  The mountains' silvan towers ;
And with the mattock, scythe and share,
  Laid low the friendless flowers.

The Woodnymphs and the Oreads, shocked
  At such dire desecration,
Caught up their blackened skirts, and fled
  Their ancient habitation,
And left the spoilers to pursue
  Their chopping and their charring,—
Complete, in short, their perfect work
  Of universal marring !

But, by and by, when things were grown
  Almost beyond enduring ;

And Nature's wounds seemed past all hope
    Of stanching, much less, curing ;
There came a Fairy to the vale,
    Of most enchanting presence,
And softly stole a gracious spell
    Upon the artless peasants.

Her smile was like the purple sheen
    That plays on lake and river,
When laughing ripples glance the shafts
    From Morning's rosy quiver ;
Her voice as sweet as sweetest harp's
    The Summer wind just kisses ;
And witching as the lays that charmed
    *The comrades of Ulysses.

She taught them that the moiling swain
    May find sufficient leisure
To nurse a sense of outward grace,
    To thrill with inward pleasure ;
And that, in all the walks of life,
    It is our bounden duty,
So far as in us lies, to veil
    A blemish with a beauty.

They heard and heeded well the words
    That clearest Truth reflected,
Whose simple logic rarely fails
    To make her laws respected ;

And soon the outraged vale began
  To show a smart improvement ;
For manly vigor followed up,
  As woman led the movement.

To blots and blemishes anon
  The change proved comi-tragic—
Old eyesores vanished from the scene,
  As if by force of magic ;
The barn no longer with the home
  Stood elbowing for precedence ;
But meekly showed its sense of right,
  By complaisant recedence.

The stable stole behind the barn ;
  Remoter still, the swine-yard ;
The door-yard spurned its further use
  Of chopping-place and kine-yard :
While cart, sled, buggy, kennel, coop,
  Decorum's hardened scorners,
Turned tail, and hid themselves away
  In proper holes and corners.

At last the Old House rubbed its eyes,
  And blushed to see how shabby
It needs must look in gabardine
  So threadbare, torn, and drabby ;
And thereupon it set to work
  With earnest perseverance,

Like tattered beau resolved to show
A downright spruce appearance.

Old clapboard lesions straight were healed ;
Old shingles sloughed their mosses ;
New panes, instead of scarecrow hats,
Made good the window's losses ;
And where the sun's rude eye till then
Had glared its bold intrusion,
Green blinds their welcome shadows dropt
Upon the dear seclusion.

And vines were planted by the door,—
The woodbine or clematis,—
To curtain in the rustic porch,
And drape the airy lattice ;
And trees of graceful form and leaf
Soon waved along all highways,
And sent their verdant juniors forth
To farthest lanes and byways

So well, that e'en at highest noon,
When June's keen solstice blazes,
And not a Sylph in all the sky
Her silvery sunshade raises,
From end to end of that fair vale,
Where'er one's promenadings,
He threads long arbors fresh and cool
With elm and maple shadings.

Yon stream that makes our native vales
  A rival land of Goshen,
Erst gathered in its myriad rills
  And bore them back to ocean ;
Unused in all its willowy course
  By groves of pines and beeches,
Save where the Indian's birch canoe
  Went idling down the reaches.

But *now*, where near-confronting hills
  Oppose their jutting shoulders,
Or rended crags have lined the shore
  With dam-inviting boulders ;
Behold, the valemen's cunning hands,
  The struggling Samson binding,
Bend his blind strength to countless tasks
  Of spinning, forging, grinding !

And what a nobler triumph still,
  When from the full-urned mountains
They won for garden, park, and lawn,
  The flash and plash of fountains ;
And bade the boon, for rich and poor
  Exhaustlessly upwelling,
A pure and sure Bethesda bide
  In every village dwelling !

And whereas, erst, no careless soul
  In all those mangled bowers,

E'er waked to give one kindly thought
    To Eden's exiled flowers ;
There's scarce a cotter now, but will,
    By dint of harder toiling,
Find time to cherish these dear waifs
    Of Adam's garden-spoiling.

Nor has his home-parterre engrossed
    His hard-earned leisure solely ;
Fondly he helps to dress the scene
    By kindred dust made holy ;
Till 'mid the verdure and the bloom
    That veil life's last dark portal,
He almost smiles to view the bourne
    'Twixt mortal and immortal.

And lo ! how fair the public taste,
    To match the general brightness,
Has robed the village church near by,
    In stole of saintly whiteness,
Which, thus arrayed, may well beseem
    To eyes of pensive weepers,
The earthly tent of angels sent
    To guard the silent sleepers.

Thus Grace and Dryad came again,
    And with them came the Muses,
Whose blessed office is to teach
    That life's true aims and uses

Are not best shown in massing gold,
  Or multiplying acres,
Nor lending sacrilegious hands
  To beauty's image-breakers ;

But in the culture of the mind,
  The soul's divine emotions,
Love, faith, peace, sympathy with all
  Heroic self-devotions ;
With reverence for genuine worth,
  No matter what the station
Of him who lifts a human heart
  To angel aspiration.

And just as Nature's face improved,
  Improved her votaries' faces,
Grown faithful mirrors to reflect
  Her humanizing graces ;
While gentle manners so prevail,
  They seal the fond conviction,
That *here*, at least, the Golden Age
  Is no poetic fiction !

THE MOTHER'S HOME-CALL.

WRITTEN BY REQUEST FOR THE " BERKSHIRE JUBILEE,"
AUGUST 22 AND 23, 1844.

WE miss the swallow's graceful wing
   When Autumn leaves grow pale and sere,
But with the soft, sweet gales of Spring,
  Her purple plumes again appear :
Green isles that crown the southern main˙
  Smiled sweetly on their minstrel guest ;
Yet all their gorgeous charms were vain
  To wean her from her mountain nest.

But ye, whose truant feet have coursed
  Afar o'er alien lands and seas,
By no imperious instinct forced
  To seek for sunnier skies than these,—
Why turn *ye* not ? ah ! wherefore let
  Strange scenes your charmèd fancies bind ?
Ah ! why for long, long years forget
  The homes and hearts ye left behind ?

O spurn at last ambition's chain
  Around your better natures wrought,
Nor longer swell the eager train
  Of fame or fortune's Juggernaut !
Return, and boyhood's faded Spring
  Shall bloom round manhood's homeward track ;
And memory's refluent sunshine fling
  The shadow from life's dial back !

The grove's lone aisles shall ring again
  With music of their vernal choirs,
While gaily on from glen to glen
  The wild brooks sweep their silvery lyres ,
And love shall ply her tenderest art,
  Sweet home her sweetest aspect wear,
That wearied mind and wounded heart
  May find a sure Bethesda there.

Come seek the scenes of boyish glee,
  The haunts of youth's sedater hours ;
And, dearer yet, the trysting-tree
  Still sweet with love's immortal flowers.
Come muse where oft in years gone by,
  O'er kindred dust ye bent the knee ;
And feel 'twere scarcely death to die,
  If their last couch your own might be !

RESPONSE OF THE RECALLED.

HAIL, Land of Green Mountains! whose val-
leys and streams
Are fair as the Muse ever pictured in dreams;
Where the stranger oft sighs with emotion sincere:
"Ah, would that my own native home had been
here!"

Hail, Land of the lovely, the equal, the brave,
Never trod by the foe, never tilled by the slave;
Where the lore of the world to the hamlet is
brought,
And speech is as free as the pinions of thought.

But blest as thou art, in our youth we gave ear
To Hope when she whispered of prospects more
dear;
Where the hills and the vales teem with garlands
untold,
And the rainbow ne'er flies with its jewels and
gold!

Yet chide not too harshly thy truants, grown gray
In the chase of bright phantoms that lured us
    astray ;
For weary and lone has our pilgrimage been
From the haunts of our childhood, the graves of
    our kin.

Nor deem that with us, out of sight out of mind
Were the homes and the hearts we left saddened
    behind,
As the hive to the bee, as her nest to the dove,
These, these have been ever our centre of love.

Yes, when far away from thee, Land of our birth,
We have mused mid the trophies and Tempes of
    earth,
Our thoughts, like thy spring-birds flown home o'er
    the sea,
In day-dreams and night-dreams have still been
    with thee.

LIFE BEYOND LIFE.

WE walked the grand old halls
　　　　From whose walls,
In the golden sunset's wane,
Looked down the pride of Spain,
Whom the pencil's magic dyes,
Warm as Andalusian skies,
Had embalmed, in age or prime,
　　　　For all time.

Far round, from antique frames,
　　　　Courtly dames,
Señoritas, young and bright
(Conscious queens in beauty's right),
Sceptred monarch, kneeling page,
Mitred priest, and civic sage,
Knight, and bard of famous lays,
　　　　Met our gaze.

In this presence of the dead,
　　　　Then I said

To my cowled and noary guide :
        What a dream is human pride !
Life's poor sands, how few and fast !
Painted phantoms of the past,
How your lips of vanished breath
        Whisper DEATH ! "

' Ah, no, my son ; no, no ;
        Say not so ! "
The old man gently sighed,
This is life to life denied !
These are victors over DEATH,
Hence to breathe immortal breath !
We the dreams, the phantoms we,
        Ay de mi ! "

LINES

TO A FRIEND, WITH LATE CHRYSANTHEMUMS.

THE sunlight falls on hill and dale
　　With slanter beam and fainter smile,
And brown leaves fleck the fitful gale,
　　Where warbling pinions glanced erewhile.

Yet these fair forms of orient race
　　Still graced my garden's faded bowers,
And lent to Autumn's mournful face
　　The charm of Summer's rosy hours.

When hope forsook the dying year,
　　They, fond and faithful to the last,
Remained, like funeral friends, to cheer
　　The void from which the loved had passed.

Thus, lady, when life's lated blight
　　Has paled thy dimples' rosy glow,
Has dimmed thy glances' starry light,
　　And flecked thy raven locks with snow,

Shall love, like these fair lingerers, seem
  Still lovelier than its vanished prime ;
And gild with purer, holier beam,
  The waste of beauty's Autumn time !

TO WILLIE.

CHILD of my failing years,
  Strength is denied me
On through life's hopes and fears
  Farther to guide thee !
Yet though *hands* fall apart,
  Loving souls, never ;
Faithful and true of heart
  Death cannot sever !

Thou must go hence *alone*,
  Whether thy path lead
Roughly o'er stock and stone,
  Smoothly through velvet mead ;
Heartened, that rough and smooth,
  Watcher and sleeper,
Castle, and cot, and booth,
  Have the same Keeper !

Strive not for wealth, but right—
  Wealth winged for fleeing !

Helpless, from night to light,
  Came we on being ;
Helpless, from light to night,
  We must go—whither?
Riches and fame and might
  Follow not thither.

Who holds, in deed and word,
  All men his neighbors ;
And, called of Christ our Lord,
  Rests from his labors,
His works do follow him
  Through the dark portal ;
Bless him and hallow him,
  Mortal immortal !

MISERERE.

ALAS, poor anxious breast !
   There seems nor peace nor rest
 On earth for thee—
No hope, no rest, no peace,
Of trouble no surcease,
  While life shall be !

I yearn unto the stars,
As through cold prison-bars,
  So stern, so strong ;
But from the pitiless sky
There cometh no reply
  To my " how long ! "

If o'er life's hither track
To youth I falter back,
  What waits me there,
But dust of perished flowers,
Spectres of murdered hours,
  Remorse, despair ?

Ah me ! how fain, how fain
Would I begin again
   That hither way ;
Whence oft my heedless soul
From duty's forthright goal
   Was lured astray !

But, Fate ! thou wilt not give
The lost years to relive,
   The past, repass ;
For vital sands, once run,
No power beneath the sun
   Can turn the glass.

Then let the precious few,
Unwasted yet, fall true
   To duty all ;
That with the last, one tear,
Spontaneous and sincere,
   For me may fall.

WHEN ?

WHEN shall this wan, wayworn Mortal,
   Heir of sorrow, pain, decay,
Reach, at last, the friendly portal
   Where all burdens fall away ?

Shall it be, when from her palace
   Smiles the morning's roseate queen ?
Or when noon with brimming chalice
   Floods the world with dazzling sheen ?

Or when day's tumultuous clamor
   Flies the weary haunts of men,
In the starry hush and glamour
   Of the night, shall it be then ?

Truce to vain interrogation !—
   Whoso to his steps gives heed,
And through travail and temptation
   Firmly follows duty's lead ;

Lifts the fallen, stays the erring,
    Wins the hopeless from despair,—
All he can on all conferring,—
    Why should he mind When or Where?

LINES TO CLARA.

'VE gazed on forms whose faultless mold
  Seemed lent from perfect worlds above,
And yet my heart, unmoved and cold,
  Repelled the glow of love ;
And thus, while others fondly praised
  Thy beauty and thy grace divine,
With stoic pride I careless gazed,
  Nor bowed before thy shrine :

Nor was the spell that binds me now,
  A willing victim to thy thrall,
Born of the locks that round thy brow
  In wreathèd darkness fall ;
Nor of the dimpled loveliness
  Of cheeks as tinted, pure and fair,
As the first rose that blooms to bless
  The Spring's maternal care :

Nor of the beams divinely bright,
  That play within thy clear dark eyes,

Like starry brilliances that light
  The gloom of midnight skies :
Not all thy dower of native charms,
  Nor all thy trophies won from. art,
Could furnish love with forceful arms
  Against my guarded heart.

But when, like some frost-stricken flower,
  The brightest in the fields of May,
Thy gentle sister, hour by hour,
  Seemed fading fast away ;
And thou, with sleepless care forlorn,
  Didst watch beside her couch of pain
From darkling eve till brightening morn,
  From morn till eve again :

Then was ambition's tyrant helm
  Struck down from manhood's passioned
        throne,
And o'er my heart's recovered realm,
  Love made thee queen alone !
There shalt thou reign, whatever lot
  Be mine on time's eventful stream ;
The theme of every waking thought,
  And every visioned dream.

TO CLARA AND AGNES.

HOMEWARD as I came last night,
   Through the wintry twilight gray,
Chanced I on as sweet a sight
   As I ever saw in May.

'Twas a little Summer scene
   In the lap of Winter placed ;
Like oasis fresh and green,
   In a dreary frozen waste.

All beneath a glassy roof,
   Though the snows around were piled,
In its covert, winter-proof,
   Sweet the little Eden smiled.

Then I blest the florist's care,
   And I praised his happy skill,
Who, when all was bleak and bare,
   Could have store of flowers at will.

And I thought, how all might take
   Lessons from the floral sage ;

And, with prudent forecast, make
  Summer grace the frosts of age ;

Make a greenhouse in the breast
  For the flowers of hope and love,
Till the gardens of the blest
  Ope to welcome them above !

DREAM OF RENT SHACKLES.

EFORE my eyes, dream-haunted in repose,
   Slowly a mighty colosseum rose ;
With which confronted, that by Tiber piled
Were but the tiny doll-house of a child.
And as I gazed the circling vastness, lo !
Came thronging in from all the winds that blow,
An ebon multitude of every age,
As if all Slavedom were on pilgrimage
To some blest shrine, where scourge and chain at
     last
Should fall forever, once its threshold passed.

Forlorn yet eager-eyed, the clanking files
Swarmed the broad arches, climbed the spacious
     aisles,
Till all the living crater, height o'er height,
In dumb expectance, wonder-struck my sight.
Then (so the dream ran) from a central dais
There rose a man, upon whose earnest face,
Homely and careworn, shone in every line
The human reflex of a soul divine,

And cried :   " Henceforth, through all the years to
        be,
By Freedom rescued, as her sons be free ! "
And as the fiat on the silence swept,
Instant from every limb the shackle leapt,
Down-clanging thunderous, as a brazen height
Shivered to atoms by a Titan's might ;
While, like an outburst of the storm-swept sea,
Swelled the wild pæan : " Free ! Forever Free ! "

SALT RIVER.

A SIGHT to behold is Salt River !
   Where Grant, with his finishing licks,
Left the chivalry all of a shiver,
   Like ghosts by the under-world Styx.

The stream—but 'tis all a misnomer
   To call it a stream, I wis—
Would baffle the genius of Homer
   To picture it just as it is :

No zephyr its surface e'er dimples ;
   No gay fins, up darting, there glance ;
No whispering leafage bewimples
   Its desolate, dreary expanse.

Dark reaches of ooze-blackened sedges
   The hideous shores make more foul,
While thunder-scarred, lichenless ledges
   Athwart the weird ugliness scowl.

As I gazed at these terrible features,
  Blue gleaming in sulphurous light,
A hulk, crammed with woe-begone creatures,
  Loomed near and more near on my sight.

The craft, to my wondering vision,
  A cross seemed 'twixt mud-scow and raft ;
Propelled by rude gusts of derision,
  And simooms of curses right aft,

Which fluttered the half-mast *Palmetto*,
  Where symbolized reptiles abhorred
Made one think of a snake-lazaretto,
  With grim death acoil in each ward.

But the crowd of the Salt River clipper
  Eclipsed in forlornness its flag,—
From Lee up to Davis, the skipper,
  And down to Toombs, Hampton and Bragg :

All solemn and silent as dummies,
  Chop-fallen, cadaverous elves,
They looked just like galvanized mummies
  Dismissed to rebury themselves.

As they faded from sight in the distance,
  There pealed a tremendous guffaw :
" Make room for the perjured resistants
  Of liberty, loyalty, law !

" Ay, room for the too long respited
    From wrath's pandemonian rod—
Let the traitors to Man be requited,
    As erst were the traitors to God!"

CAPITOLIAN SOLILOQUY.

SO Lincoln's dead, and *I* now President !—
  The ways of Providence are dark indeed ;
But sages, peering through the gloom, discern
That they do often lead to shining ends.
Beyond the dead Chief, fallen in his tracks
While groping onward with uncertain feet,
I see a beckoning splendor like the morn's !
He was too gentle, too infirm of will,
To meet the stern exactions of the time ;
And so the patient Wisdom that o'er-rules
Men's faults and failings for the general good,
Removed him, as was meet ; and in his stead,
Set one who hath no woman in his soul,
When Justice girds him with her awful brand.
Well may ye shrink and tremble at the flash
Of its impending vengeance ! ye who've filled
The fairest land whereon the sun e'er shone,
With deeper gloom than all its forests shed
Before the axe first smote their boundless aisles.
Behold the desolation ye have wrought—
The countless graves your bloody hands have filled

With martyrs battling for the rights of man,—
Ay, even *yours*, who slew them with the sword,
Or gave them, bound, to famine's sharper bale !
Behold the widows by a thousand hearths,
The widowed sweethearts—never to be wives—
From whose forlornness hope shall ne'er beguile
The sackcloth and the ashes of despair !
Behold the myriad heroes halt and maimed,
That but for your demoniac hate, had still
Sustained the feeble, faltering steps of age ;
And not themselves, in manhood's broken prime,
Been shamed, the stalwart on the weak to lean !
These are the wrecks and ruins ye have wrought,
Traitors ! and were my hand to stay the scourge
That should make treason odious, and yourselves
Abhorred, methinks the very stones would leap,
The groves rush forward with their outstretched
    rods,
To wreak the justice man had failed to do.

What was that whispered in my ear but now :
" Vengeance is sweet, but sweeter far is power " ?
Get thee behind me, Tempter !—Yet who knows
'Twas not the wiser second thought that spake ?
If I do smite the smitten, make them take
The back seat in the temple they profaned,
They'll storm or sulk, nor lend a beggar's staff
To keep me steady on the lofty dais
To which assassination cleared my way.

But, say I turn my back upon myself,
Ignore the brave words fulmined at their crimes,
Ignore my solemn promises to those
Whose faith and favor made me what I am,
Forgive the babblers that proclaimed me boor,
And hug the dear, good friends, whose fingers
    itched
To have my weasand in their ready noose,—
Why, then, if there be any grace at all
In democratic bosoms, South or North,
The alienated brothers *must* strike hands,
Fall on each other's neck with joyful tears,
And make the author of their making-up
The happiest sequence of an accident
In all the pregnant histories of chance !

INSURANCE ECHOES!
SAINT PROMETHEUS.

EACH Guild a sainted patron claims,
  And strives his praise to show forth—
Saint George, Saint Pat, Saint Nick, Saint
    James,
  Saint Jonathan and so forth :
But *ours*, we hold, must stand confest,
  Among all haloed actors,
The grandest, blandest, brilliantest
  Of sainted benefactors.

What but for his high-handed act
  Were now our genial planet,
But one inhospitable tract
  Of glacial drift and granite?
With here and there a smokeless hut,
  Where clods with human features
Lay hybernating, stark (all but),
  As Greenland's torpid creatures.

Fire is the nutriment we crave,
  Yet crave in modest courses ;

A *little* makes us strong and brave,
  A surfeit saps our forces ;
Our eyeballs flash with lurid gleams
  From fate's volcanic crashes,
And all our golden hopes and dreams
  Are turned to dust and ashes !

Therefore, dear Saint, give wise dissent
  To unrestrained fruition ;
We flourish most in time of Lent,
  But perish of repletion ;
So, when your bounty falls our way,
  As fate or chance disposes,
Dispense your fiery favors, pray,
  In homœopathic doses !

But not on *self* alone to build,
  Your salamandrine cravers,
For our Big Brothers of the Guild
  Implore coequal favors—
Ay ! patriarchal days for those
  Who, ware of Time's reverses,
Prevent their darlings' future woes
  By drafts on present purses.

To Beauty still give starry eyes,
  And soft sheet-lightning glances ;
And in her lover's tropic sighs,
  Melt all her frosty fancies ;
To Hymen's torch give steadier sheen,
  More pure, celestial splendor,

Than earth has seen since Eden's queen
    Made love's first soul-surrender.

" This sensible warm being " is
    The boon of your bestowing—
Oh, keep, in veins and arteries,
    The vital currents flowing !
Let Health the silver cords of life
    Make long and strong as cables,
To mock the grim old Scyther's knife,
    And Carlisle's mortal tables.

Why should Time's later children's breath,
    Alas ! be so uncertain ?
Scarce step we on the stage, ere Death
    Lets fall the sable curtain ;
Whereas, as every school-boy knows,
    The patriarchs would have wondered
At Juliets sparked by Romeos,
    Before their second hundred !

Let Medicine's modern fountains, then,
    Make real Ponce de Leon's ;
And life's poor three score years and ten
    Claim kinship with the eons ;
While premiums pour so free and fast,
    As countless patrons rain them,
That, like the wondrous " books," at last,
    The world could scarce contain them !

THE POETRY OF FIRE INSURANCE.

"SOME dreamers maintain, as a matter of
  fact,
That this marvelous wide world contains not a
    tract,
Not a nooklet, so utterly blasted and bare,
That a poet can't still find some beauty-spot there.

" How often, as Bruce and his Nubian band
In their ' desert-ships ' toiled over oceans of sand,
Some flower of the waste, like a waif from the
    skies,
Thrilled their souls to the quick with a joyous sur-
    prise !

"When Kane made his home on that desolate
    shore
Unmarked by the footprint of mortal before,
Gay mosses upsmiled from perennial snows,
And budded and bloomed where his quicksilver
    froze.

"And they hold that the truth of this thesis ob-
    tains
As widely in man's as in nature's domains ;
That the Muse never found so degraded a race,
Where she could not discern *some* æsthetical trace.

"Well, the Seminole's hut, or the Hottentot's
    kraal,
Perchance may some faint sense of beauty re-
    call ;
But I'd fain like to know what poetical thrill
Was ever yet due to a Policy-mill ? "

And you *shall* know, anon, my incredulous friend,
If those rather tall ears to my wisdom you'll
    lend ;
For the theme is as full, this respondent conceives,
Of poetical charms, as a rosebud of leaves :

Whatever is lofty in nature or art ;
Whatever is lovely in mind or in heart ;
Whate'er, though of earth, is unearthy—behold,
There Poetry points to her placers of gold !

Take the apposite case of the Asbestos Co.,
With its surplus, say *One*, with five ciphers in tow,
Whence the Board, every half year, is free to de-
    clare
Ten to twenty per cent.—isn't there poetry there ?

Lucretius has sung of the landman's delight,
To stand all secure on some ocean-chafed height,
And see, while the tempest remorselessly raves,
The mariner tossed on the perilous waves.

But who the poetical rapture can tell,
Of a President, roused by the City Hall bell
To some warehouse in flames, as he chuckles :
    "O-ho !
Our policy there expired some hours ago ! "

And there's poetry, too, of that quizzical kind
By critical experts SATIRIC defined,
As he says to his friend : " If the truth were but
    known,
" *Your* policy then took the place of our own !

" For the broker, whose favor your Board still en-
    dures,
Went straight, we perceived, from our counter to
    yours ;
We felt rather vexed of the risk to be reft,
But our loss, o'er the right, proves your gain, o'er
    the left ! "

When a Chatham Street queer-nose, from Pesth or
    Cracow,
" Vants ein bolice on sthock in mein sthore," so and
    so ;

How tempers poetical license the shock
Of refusal, with " Sir, we are full on that block."

Just see how the answer would look in plain
      prose :
" There's the door, you can vanish—we don't fancy
      those
Whose catskins turn beaver, whose pinchbeck, fine
      gold,
If a spark, ten doors off, they but chance to be-
      hold ! "

But, friends of the Guild, to leave jesting apart,
And return to the sober concerns of our art ;
I am free to declare, as my settled belief,
That we're not only poets, but poets in chief.

Let Fame call her roll of the Lords of the lyre,
Who for ages have stood at the head of the choir ;
And our brilliant Parnassus shall answer her thus :
Stuff and nonsense ! they can't hold a candle to
      us !

Mass all the grand epics the trade ever sold
(Your Homers, your Dantes), in tissues of gold ;
And the expert whose home the Red demon de-
      vours
Wouldn't take the whole lot for his five lines of
      ours.

He has but to mention our two-leaved brochure—
That poem of poems : " Do HEREBY INSURE,"
And, presto ! the nightmare of ruin takes flight,
Like goblin caught napping by morn's sudden light.

No matter how far his "burnt district " may be
From the Guild, whose long arms reach from centre
       to sea ;
He has only to whisper our magical strain,
And what was, but is not, has being again.

While the embers yet gleam and the smoke eddies
       still
O'er the site of his mansion, shop, warehouse, or
       mill,
Their doubles return large as life to his view,
And all, Phœnix-like, from their ashes brand-new.

Talk of authors renowned in the poetry line
For their odes, and their pæans, and epics divine ;
Why, our numbers long since even Milton's dis-
       crowned—
For *one* Paradise lost, we've writ myriads *found!*

THE SAMSON OF THE HEARTH.

ONCE on a time there was a mighty man
    Whose strength was in his locks, until his
       foes
Found out their secret, and with glozing wiles
Lured them away ; and then the mighty one
Became a very infant in their hands.
Yet, mindful of his prowess in the past,
They held him firmly bound, nor felt secure
Till they had quenched his sight in utter gloom.
And even then his presence awed them so,
They shrank to spurn him with their coward feet
While prone in dust, or grinding at the mill,
Daily and all day long, in blind despair.
But when his shredded locks were grown again,
And his tormentors, wild with insolent mirth,
Made him the target of their gibes and jeers,
He seized the pillars that upheld the fane,
Profaned by their inhuman ribaldries,
And, with one wrench of his resistless might,
Buried the mockers and the mocked in death !

I, FIRE, am fellow of that vengeful slave ;
I, the Sun-born ! to whom my bright sire gave
The strength and glory of his own proud locks,
And bade me share my gifts with all his worlds.
Thought-swift, I glance from circling orb to orb,
And, with the genial splendor of my smile,
Clothe hill, vale, peak, cloud, lake, and billowy
    sea.
To all the infinite forms within my scope
I bring free largess ; germ and bulb and root,
Blind worm, and torpid chrysalis, feel my touch
The wand of life ; the meadows laugh, the woods
And orchards loose their buds to leaves, and flowers,
And fruits,—the vital gems in Flora's crown.
But man, the insatiate tyrant, in whose heart
Even these rich guerdons leave an aching void,
Conspired my thraldom, and with subtle arts
Hath brought me into bondage to his will.
What is the task he does not put me to—
Me, the Sun-born ?   For him *I* grind and groan,
Like my blind brother of the fateful locks ;
I am his vassal of the caverned mine,
The clanging forge, the thund'rous battle-field ;
For him I melt the stubborn rocks to streams
Of preciousness ineffable ; I flash
His wants and wishes, instant, round the world ;
Drive his great argosies from zone to zone ;
And hold the torch that guides their darkling way
Along the perilous clash of surge and shore.

Ay, what the task he does not put me to?
I am his moiling chattel of all work ;
But most of all, the bond-slave of his hearth.
There, when from earliest morn to latest eve,
I've cheered his home with comfortable warmth,
And light, and gladness, and have blest his board
With viands meet to tempt the taste of gods—
Even there and then, the ingrate heaps my locks
With stifling ashes, and, without a thank
Or careless "good-night," yawns him off to bed !
Then have I time, as ever the fierce will,
To study vengeance on my slumbering foe.
Unwatched, I watch keen-eyed, and pry.and peer
For chink or cranny in my prison-wall ;
And long and listen for the robber's stealth,
Or wind's, or rodent's—ay, for anything
To loose me from these contumelious bonds,
And cricket mockers of my smothered wrath.
Nor always long in vain ! for Accident,
Though shooting wildly without mark or aim,
Hath such exhaustless quiver to his bow,
He needs must send a random shaft at last
Just where my wishes pioneered its flight !
And when his lucky arrow hath set free
My fettered limbs, I seize on aught that makes
For sure enlargement—joist, or stud, or beam—
And ever climbing roofward, fling anon
My flaming banner to the rallying winds.
Ashes for ashes, tyrants ! on *your* heads,

Lo, *now* the gray dishonors pressed on mine !
Peal your loud larums, all your powers combine
To stay the unbound Samson of the hearth !
Ha ! how I mock your frantic energies,
I, the Sun-born ! as with resistless might
I trample your fair homes to smoldering dust ;
Trample the garnered riches of all climes,
And the vast piles they choked from crypt to
    dome ;
Ay, and the very temples of your gods,
Where your young brows were hallowed at the font,
Your wedded vows sealed sweet with orange-
    blooms,
And whence, in pallor and with dirge and knell,
Wept or unwept, ye pass from mortal sight !

Thus do I visit vengeance on my foes !
Thus smite their braveries with my crimson
    scourge !
Sleepless, I watch and wait the time and chance
To magnify the might of my dread locks,
In fierce requital of the hoary wrongs,
Shames, and serf-shackles I have borne from men.
" Ashes for ashes ! " is the script I write,—
I, the Sun-born,—upon the human waste,
The double desert of their homes and hopes !

SAFE AND SOUND.

NIGHT.

A SUBURBAN VILLA.

SOLIDUS *at a desk covered with papers.*

HERE ! I have carefully gone o'er
    From first to last the precious store,
And found my evening's labor crowned
With the old joy, " *All Safe and Sound !* "
Men risk their thousands on a ship,
That, in the first storm's frantic grip,
May be o'erwhelmed or dashed ashore
' Mid crash and shriek and brakers' roar.
Men build their millions into walls
Of temples, castles, villas, halls,
For Time's slow mills (that rest nor rust !)
To grind into their primal dust.
And whose the vast statistic lore
Can sum the mighty millions more
Sown broadcast in the fields of life,
For comfort, culture, peace or strife ?

Of all the sower's varied seed
How scant the harvest ! if, indeed,
The cast do not so luckless fall,
No harvest waits his hand at all !
His streams give out, or dams give way ;
His workmen strike for higher pay ;
His factories burn, or boilers burst ;
His railroads grow from worse to worst
With wear and tear and service slack,
And cars alert to jump the track
And rush their living freight to death,
Or mulcts whose vastness stops his breath ;
His agents filch, his bankers fail,
His clerks and factors take leg-bail ;
His gold and gilt-edged turn to dross—
How oft his gains are gains of loss !

Now, look at these Insurance stocks !
Here's stanchness !—here, indeed, are " *rocks,*"
Whose calm stability derides
The utmost brunt of time and tides ;
While from their generous lap descends
A brilliant stream of dividends.
Who would not have a vested right
In such a fountain of delight
His pocket's present thirst to suage,
And mock the keener drouth of age ?
Scarce than an angel seems he less,
Who, in his depths of consciousness

(As in the block the sculptor sees
The statue that all eyes shall please),
First saw Insurance, and straightway
Revealed her glories to the day.
Insurance—that which makes one sure,
Firm, fearless, stable, safe, secure !
What else of all life's fond pursuits
Is blest with half these attributes ?
And *where* does any mortal know
The peer of our ASBESTOS Co.;
With capital of mammoth size,
And surplus marvelous likewise ?
Then, too, its corps of officers—
All nonpareil philosophers,—
With grandest gift of second-sight
To pierce the future's blackest night :
They saw Chicago's latent flame
Long years before the outburst came ;
Saw its vast piles in ruin fall,
And desolation brooding all,
Where pealed, but now, the din of trade,
And life seemed one long masquerade—
They saw it all with wise alarm,
And kept a thousand miles from harm ;
So that when burst the fire-storm there,
No scrip of theirs got singed a hair !

O seers of ashes yet to be !
O pets of perspicacity !

Ye were too serpent-shrewd by far
To be befooled as myops are ;
Or lured, like moths, to dire distress
By risks of dazzling speciousness !
As charity begins at home,
Your "lines " all hug the State-House dome,
That from its sov'reign height looks down
On every inch of Boston town.
Its streets are, sooth, but winding lanes
Vertiginous to stranger brains ;
But then for width they make amends
By peaks that court the clouds for friends ;
Each member of the massive pile
Made grander with his Mansard " tile."
There Commerce heaps her varied store,
In compact millions, floor on floor,
Whence living streams of premiums flow
To our world-famed AsBESTOS Co.
True, rates are low, commissions high,
And competition sharp and spry ;
But, then, the Hub may justly boast,
Each Red-Shirt is himself a host,
Each engine a tamed cataract,—
Niagara on wheels, in fact ;
Where every risk is granite-clad
(Safer old Petra never had !) ;
Where products of stupendous worth
Of all the industries of earth
May fire and flame as calmly brave
As merman in his deep-sea cave.

But hark !—what does that newsboy cry ?
" Boston all burning ? "—What a lie !—
(Kling, ling !)—Ah ! here's a telegram.

(*Messenger, aside.*)

Guess boss'll *think*, if not say, damn ! "
(*Reads.*)

" Boston in flames from end to end !—
Whole blocks in ashes !—worse, my friend :
Our venerable ASBESTOS CO.
Went up (no, down) an hour ago !—
Its scrip not worth a copper's toss ;
Claimants—we can't pay half their loss ! "

Saddle my swiftest, ho, you, sir !
I must to town, John, whip and spur !
Fire may, perhaps, melt granite blocks,
But that my staid Insurance stocks
To ashes could be made to fall
(Asbestos ashes least of all !)
Is matter for supreme surprise ;
See it I must with my own eyes,
Or hold it but a fable, though
With her own lips Truth swear, 'Tis so !

THE PROMETHEAN FLAME.

WHEN, long, long ago, on Olympus sublime
  Gods and goddesses led a right jolly old
   time,
With nectar for champagne, ambrosia for bread,
And amaranths crowning each aureoled head,
As they feasted and chatted o'er partisan leagues,
Or gave the bright hours to erotic intrigues,
They had no more regard for poor humans down
  here,
Than our city gods have for the muttons they shear.

At last it befel that Iapetus' son,
Whose heart took no part in this frolic and fun,
Gazed mournfully far through the nether abyss,
As an angel might gaze on the exiled from bliss.
Say, wherefore do tears dim those piteous eyes?
Ah, why should the breast of a god heave with
  sighs?
Would you know? on the pinions of Fancy take
  flight,
And see for yourself what so saddened his sight.

Lo, Earth lies before you in horror outspread,
Cold, ghastly, and still, as the face of the dead ;
Her mountains all swathed in parennial snows,
Whose pallor the morn scarcely flushes with rose ;
No peak to the night its red banner uplifts,
Or with smoke veils the glare of its pinnacled
  drifts ;
No surge breaks in thunder on sea-wall or shore,
For the vast of her oceans is ice to the core ;
And the murmur of rivers, the outlaugh of rills,
No longer rejoices her valleys and hills ;
While her cataracts, fast in weird fetters of frost,
In a trance of white silence their voices have lost.

Then he, from whose heart the warm tears had up-
  welled,
As this desolate waste of a world he beheld,
Cried fondly : "O Lord of Olympus ! restore
The light of thy smile to yon outcast once more .
Ah, see how Spring, Summer, and Autumn are fled
From the scenes where their beauty and blessings
  were shed !
While Winter has stretched his usurping domains
North to South, South to North, over green hills
  and plains,
Till stark o'er the tropics his cold sceptre gleams,
And but *one* zone now links the far polar extremes !
Oh, pity thy low-lying children of Earth,
As in torpor they dream by the emberless hearth,

Whence no smoke-wreath by day, no dear glimmer
　　by night
Gives token of comfort or social delight ,
And the voice of affection in cottage and hall,
Is still as the cold lips low under the pall !
Save a moan here and there, all thy Earth-world is
　　dumb—
No peal of the bugle, no roll of the drum,
No ring of the anvil, no hum of the mill,
No cheer of blithe labor from valley or hill,
No roar of thronged cities, no pathos of prayer,
Sends a thrill to the soul of the desolate air.

" Ah, lord of all worlds and their dwellers ! be-
　　hold
Thine altars are flameless, thy censers are cold ;
No garlanded victim is led to thy doors ;
No chalice its sacred libation outpours ;
And Flamen and Vestal, o'erwhelmed by thy scorn,
In pallor and darkness lie mute and forlorn.
Oh, questionless monarch of mortals and gods !
Have pity at last on these human-faced clods ;
With thy bright boon of fire hallow dwelling and
　　fane,
And let Earth's palsied wastes thrill with rapture
　　again ! "

Alas ! like the dew on some sand-smothered space,
Or the cloud's flying kiss on the crag's iron face,

Fell the voice of the pleader on Jove's careless ear ;
For it chanced that, just then, a young goddess
    smiled near,
And of course his High-mightiness could not bestow
A thought on his victims there under the snow.

Indignant to find that his merciful zeal
Could win no response to his yearning appeal,
He snatched a live brand from the god's golden
    hearth,
And sped the bright spoil toward the dolorous Earth.
Ere he touched her cold bosom, its life-kindling rays
Have set her extinguished volcanoes ablaze ;
And the long-silenced voice of her ice-cumbered
    streams
Breaks out, like a bird's, in the rapture of dreams ;
While the great heart of Ocean, transpierced by the
    glow
Of that meteor-flame, feels a jubilant throe ;
And hark ! how the rhythm of its pulse-beat once
    more
Sends the tidings of joy to his uttermost shore !

And see ! as from headland to headland he hies,
How the dead beacons flash their electric surprise
Far forth, far around, over offing and bay,
And Darkness, dethroned, shrinks bewildered away !
As onward he bears the glad largess of light,
All Lares grow cheery, all hearths warm and bright ;

And tea-kettles warble their long-silenced strains ;
And sparking-lamps shine for love's lingering
    swains ;
And foundry and forge smite the resonant air
With clangor, and flame, and Cyclopean glare ;
While the fierce iron-horse, as he dashes away,
Shakes the echoing hills with his terrible neigh.

As the torch-bearer bursts on this Gotham of ours,
And the genial glow, mantling turrets and towers,
Thaws the hoar that, for ages, had hidden from sight
Their red-brick and brown-stone in cerements of
    white,
Old Santa Claus, roused from his centuried spell,
Sprang up and made tracks for the City-Hall bell,
And giving full force to his vigorous arm,
Made Night hold her ears at the stunning alarm.
And, wonder of wonderful sights ! what are those
That leap like red ghosts from yon hummocks of
    snows ?
How they stare through the rime that bewimples
    their eyes !
How they beat their numb hands against thorax
    and thighs !
How they listen and count the quick strokes—
    ' three ! five ! ten ! '
Why, bless our dull wits, these are Mose and his
    men !
And hark ! with what lungs most potential of noise,
He trumpets, " Be lively now ; jump her, my boys ! "

Or, with big mouth (a good deal more open than
    shut)
Thunders, " Sikesy, you son of a snail, take the
    but ! "
And away they tear crashing o'er cobble and flag,
As if fifty spurred Dexters strained hard at the
    drag.

But the sight which the climax of wonder awoke,
Was the guild of the resurrect Policy-folk,
Of whose torpor-struck hosts not a frost-bitten soul
For ages had taken one premium toll ;
For their customers, stark in the general chill,
Sent never the ghost of a grist to the mill.
But lo ! now the wintry embargo is o'er,
How jolly the sound of the grinding once more !
For patrons and brokers are thick as you please,
And the millers, you bet, all more busy than bees,
As city and country their hoppers astound
With mountains of risks all agog to be ground !

Oh ye, whom the Bringer of Fire has thus blest,
Let his name and his fame on your hearts be im-
    prest ;
Or, rather, burnt into their innermost core,
For time to erase or deface never more.
And I move, sir, that now every glass shall be filled
To him who so specially favored our guild
With that flambeau divine, that beneficent thaw—
Three cheers for Prometheus—hip, hip, hurrah !

SONNET.

RIVER, that lingerest in thy blithe career
    From the blue mountains to the dark blue
      sea,
To list the passing-bell's stern monody,
And love's lorn wail beside the loved one's bier—
Say to the careless worldling sauntering near :
" Speak low ! step softly ! as in awe profound ;
For, know thou, this indeed is holy ground,
Planted by God for his great Harvest Year.
He will not let his seed forever lie,
Germless and dead, within the stifling mold !
Though sown in weakness, it shall safe defy
The worm, the storm, the Seasons' heat and cold ;
And, in due time, from out the dust arise
To his eternal garner of the skies ! "

SONNET.

A H, never, lady, can we hope to stand
    Acquitted debtors for the kindness done
By thee and thine to our beloved one,
When, lorn and friendless, in the alien land,
She felt the warm clasp of your gentle hand,
And heard fond words whose music seemed to be
Home's own dear echoes from beyond the sea,
Sweeter than gales from flowery Samarcand !
Oh, that, for once, were ours the magic art,
In dearth of hopeless ingots of the mine,
To coin the golden wishes of the heart,
And grace the mintage with thy face divine—
What precious stores our bosoms would impart !
What sumless coffers, lady, then were thine !

SONNET.

WHEN shall the free in name be free indeed ;
　　Nor thou, my country, blush to own us sons,
In whose degenerate bosoms coldly runs
The blood of heroes whose immortal meed
Was benison of trampled millions freed ?
Blind slaves of this or that discordant clan,
We sink the patriot in the partisan,
And shout when friends, not principles, succeed.
With sword and shield our fathers met the foe ;
With tongue and pen we battle with our brother,
· And madly strive to stigmatise each other
With uncouth names, worn threadbare long ago,
In alien clash of whig and tory creed—
Oh, when shall free-born men be free indeed !

SONNET.

TO A BEREAVED MOTHER.

BORN mother of a young Immortal, fled
 So soon from thy fond arms and wistful
 eyes !
Who shall reprove thy ever-yearning sighs,
Or bid the bitter tears remain unshed ?
He was thy first-born, and his beauty fed
Thy soul with manna from love's sweetest skies,
Nor couldst thou deem a cherub in disguise
Lay smiling on thee from his cradle bed.
Thou couldst not see, within the moulded clay,
The spirit's wings their latent splendors dart ;
Nor hear the missioned angels fondly say
To the pale shape so clasped to thy sad heart :
" A throne is waiting in the realms of day—
King of a new-born Sphere, let us depart ! "

DEAN STANLEY.

WITH grave, frank smile he took me by the
hand,
And gently earnest, drew me to his side—
He, the great scholar of renown world-wide ;
Me, all unknown even in my native land—
And as I, listening, gazed upon his face,
So wise, so winsome, yet so saintly grand,
I longed that pride the charm might understand
Of perfect goodness and unconscious grace.
Then memory whispered : " Marvel not that one,
Whose life in England's Pantheon is passed,
Should find his kindred genius clothed upon
With the effulgent glories round him cast,
　　That fill the mighty minster's solemn pile
　　From crypt to cross, as with an angel's smile ! "

THE ANABASIS.

Sursum deorsum.—Plautus.

Ὀρώρει δ'οὐρανόθεν Βοῦς.—Homer (mostly).

UGENE, and Frank, and I, three bosom-
   friends,
Stood gaily chatting by the college-door,
What time our merry mates, a furlong off,
Made the gymnasium ring with boisterous glee,
As was their wont before the evening task.
Behind the curtain of the western hills
The weary sun had sought his golden couch ;
But, eastward still, athwart the shadowed vale,
His passing glory flushed the lifted brow
'Of cloud-communing Graylock, as he stood
With all his pines on tiptoe, gazing down
Upon his brother Titan's gorgeous bed.

As gradual twilight deepened round us there
Commingling blithe discourse, the deacon's cow,
A buxom beast, stole forth upon the lawn

276

To snatch the dewy verdure, in such sort
As one by sharp experience made too wise
To *eke* fruition of forbidden fruit.
Then Frank, with roguish gravity : " My friends,
The good time coming is already come !
Our railroad age has sped improvement's car
To cot, to hovel, yea to stall and byre !
Baboons are taught to sit at festive board ;
Bruin to dance the minuet ; and I move
That yonder cow be favored with a chance
To rise above the commonwealth of kine,
And stand, sublimely ruminant, on heights
Ne'er scaled by bovine neophyte before ! "

No sooner said, than, with a smothered burst,
I seized the tether trailing from her horns ;
While Frank, like Palinurus at his helm,
Gravely officious, plied the tillered tail.
No grass, I ween, did grow beneath her feet,
Ere we had cleared the threshold with our charge ;
When taking breath, and having skyward turned
Her white-rimmed vision, up a zig-zag flight
Of four-score stairs we eased our panting prize,
From landing unto landing stumbling up,
With such reverberate racket in the void
And long-drawn corridors, as well might drown
A band of Feejee tomtoms in full thud.

Now, as it chanced, the Tutor was abroad,
But not his key, which, nimbly seized and plied,

Gave access to his sanctum in a trice.
Thither we urged his uninvited guest,
Whom leaving with the Lares, off we sped,
Each to his several chamber, sorely tasked
To smooth rebellious wrinkles, and suppress
Guffaws that wrestled with the aching ribs,
And shook the central diaphragm for vent,
As erst the prisoned winds old Æol's cave.

Soon pealed the bell for evening tasks ; but scarce
The buzzing swarm had settled in the hive,
Ere came the Tutor round from room to room,
Beseeching aid, with face all crisp with smiles :
For that a strange alumnus had made bold
To scale his lofty sanctum, and install
A most uncouth, unclassic presence there.
Anon the halls were thronged with flaring lamps,
As Pandemonium for a torch-light spree
Had mustered all its imps ; and when the shout
Excelsior echoed, up the oaken heights
Two hundred heels went thundering all at once,
Four stairs at every bound, and yells to match—
A din to make an adder hold his ears.

Just as the fore-front reached the Tutor's door,
There came a crash, as of a dome of glass
Shivered to atoms by a giant's rage ;
For when the beast, already sore amazed,
Beheld the goblin rout, and drank the glare

Of those weird lights, stark mad with panic fear,
She plunged the dizzy casement at a bound,
And swept sash, blinds and all to outer night !
But kindly fates outsped her, and received
The hairy meteor in the buoyant arms
Of a subjacent maple, where she hung
Pawing the rustling verdure, as it were
A monster floundering in a green morass.
Soon lanterns gleamed abroad, and ropes were
        plied,
And those four sturdy legs, restored to earth,
Dashed off without a limp in all their bones,
The sequent tail outstanding straight behind !

ALUMNUS AND ALMA MATER.

IN a certain quaint town o'er the Canada line,
   While "looking about," as a Yankee is wont,
I presently found myself posed to divine
   The use of a grim-visaged pile in my front.

After gazing awhile at the mystical wall,
   I bowed myself in at its fortress-like door ;
And lo ! the whole space of a half-acre hall
   Was swarming alive with an infantile corps.

For breastplates they all sported white cotton bibs
   Over pinafores fragrant with indigo blue ;
And Fancy at once fell to tickling her ribs
   With the guess of a National Baby Review.

Composing my face, till no trace of a smile
   Showed that fun ever rippled its deacon-like calm,

Quoth I to the fair chief on duty the while :
  "Are all these,—excuse me,—your children,
    madame ?"

Up flew the plump arms with : "*Ma foi, quelle mé-*
    prise !"
And a flush that almost set her coiffure ablaze—
"*Ce sont d'enfans trouvés, moi, fille de l'église,*
  Non pas mère de famille, à dieu qu'il ne plaise !"

Slight cause to get miffed, friends, had mademoi-
    selle—
For, if of a good thing one can't have too much,
One can't have too many a good thing as well,
  And, for my part, I hold that the yonkers are
    such.

(*Interrupted by a voice.*)

"So do I, too !" "And, pray, who are *you* that
    make free
  In this muddle of rhyme to adventure an oar ?"
"Why, lad, don't you know me ?" "Ah, yes, now
    I see ;
  Alma Mater ! How gladly I yield you the floor !"

"Well knew I, my son, I had only to glance
  At the place with such filial obeisance resigned,
To be favored at once with the coveted chance
  To give that prim prude there a piece of my
    mind.

" Though she's so far away, it would weary a bird
   In a day's flight to traverse the interposed scene ;
Never fear but I'd manage to make myself heard,
   Were there fifty Vermonts lying lengthwise be-
         tween.

" So, Vestal, you think yourself specially blest
   That you ne'er rocked a cradle nor sung lullaby !
How dare you, with beauty's orbed glory of breast,
   Its whole anatomical purport belie ?

"Had our foremother Eve never vouchsafed an
         heir,
   For that offspring are naught but incarnated sin,
I would fain like to ask of your sapience, ' Where
   Would her possible Adams and Eves now have
         been ? '

" From the day the first minstrel gave voice to the
         lute,
   The *flowers* have bloomed out in all manner of
         lays ;
But methinks 'twould have been quite as well if the
         fruit
   Had come in, now and then, for a part of the
         praise.

" Had you followed your mother's example, my lass,
   And been graced with the crown that to wifehood
         enures,

You wouldn't have thought my alumnus an ass
  For asking if those blessed babies are yours.

" Now just look at *me* and the honest truth speak—
  Am I not still erect, buxom, fresh, debonair ?
Would the leaf of a blush-rose, if laid to my cheek,
  Be seen, or if seen, look discountenanced there ?

" Yet the mandate, 'Be fruitful,' and so forth, for
      years
  I have strictly obeyed, nor once dreamed to
      ignore,
Till my family census at present appears
  (Here's the catalogue, Miss) above one hundred
      score !

" All boys—every one—an adelphian throng,
  For I've travailed till now but the masculine way ;
Though, perhaps, like my Oberlin sister, ere long
  I may bring in the crinolines, just for fair play :

" For if the first Coelebs went sighing, until
  A sweet chum smiled near, as we're taught by the
      muse ;
Is it strange that his celibate offspring should thrill
  At the thought of the same rosy cure for the
      blues ?

" But we'll not stop to ponder what *may* come to
      pass
  In the hopeful Hereafter that fancy foretells,

When the honors and parchments which fall to each
        class,
    Shall (a full half at least) be the spoil of its belles.

" To return to the boys—not the motherless ones,
    That your Montreal Bastile forlornly immures—
Waifs—*nullius filii*—nobody's sons,—
    No wonder you don't like to own they are yours !

" But the lads I am proud as a queen to call mine,
    As born of my loins and fain nursed at my breast,
Whose heart tendrils all with my own intertwine
    In a plexus of love, like the souls of the blest.

"What a family group were my darlings to-day,
    From the four winds recalled, at their mother's
        knee found !
The ten-acre Mission Park over the way,
    Could hardly make room for a good hug all
        round.

" Yet proud as I were such a household to greet,
    I have barely begun my maternal career ;
Just wait till I give Doctor Hopkins the treat
    To christen and bless a full hundred a year !

" And fear not my motherly means will give out,
    Though new mouths come in by the great gross
        or more ;

Not a true son of mine but will strive, never doubt,
  That Want, the gaunt wolf, shall not darken my
      door.

"Not one of them all I have sent to the field
  To bear his just part in the battle of life,
But would rather be borne to me stark on his shield,
  Than live to disgrace me by shirking the strife.

"Wherever their lines in this fair world are cast,
  No Tempe can charm like their mother's domain;
And the years in her lap with the Muses there
     passed,
  Are those they would soonest live over again!"

EAR Alma! we know you are wise as Ju-
piter's brain-mothered daughter,
And love your fair home passing well in beautiful,
dutiful Berkshire ;
But your visits so frequent of late to this wonder-
ful, thunderful Babel,
Are riddles immensely beyond the uttermost scope
of our guessing.
You surely have heard the old saw, that the rolling
stone gathers no mosses !
Do wise fellows cotton to girls whose gadding hints
holes in their stockings ?
The spinning of street-yarn is not the kind by New
England commended
In spinster or wife, and of all, least of all in her
paragon mothers.
For *you*, then, O Mater, with arms so freighted
with family pledges,
The wife of John Rogers would seem a childless
forlorn one beside you,

To wrest your dear face from them all, twitch
　　your apron-strings out of their fingers,
Bolt nursery-door and make tracks, as if from a
　　pest-house of foundlings—
Ah, Alma, for *you* to turn tramp, we couldn't have
　　dreamed such a scandal !

　It may be all right you should give tired lap,
　　arms, and bosom a respite—
No fondest of mothers quite likes to play the peren-
　　nial fountain ;
But where was the need you should seek for respite
　　and recuperation
'Mid the roar, and the rush, and the crush of this
　　metropolitan bedlam ?
Our Berkshire, for souls tempered right, is fraught
　　with serene satisfactions ;
The school-house and church, side by side, have
　　nurtured her people to cherish
The golden mean of content, next the golden rule
　　of the Master.
Her streams are the clearest that e'er were born of
　　the cloud's purest crystals ;
Than hers, never lake mirrored charm of sunsets
　　more kindred to Eden's :
In Summer her valleys and hills take captive the
　　heart of the stranger ;
In Autumn, his faith that the court of Iris here tis-
　　sues her rainbows ;

In Winter, that giants are camped from border to
    uttermost border,
Their white tents all warded the while by Greylock's
    imperial pavilion.

But, Alma, since all these delights were powerless
    to hold you to Berkshire,
Pray, what *was* the magical charm that sundered
    the matronal tether ?
We're sure it could never have been the bewildering
    glamour of fashion—
The craving to see the last styles of coiffures and
    panniers prodigious,
Wherewith the town belles so astound the vision of
    men and good angels.
Eureka ! I have it at last—you wanted to see the
    scarred veterans
You sent to the field in their prime, to push things
    for man and his rights ;
And as, in the terrible stress, they couldn't break
    ranks and go to you,
You've followed Mohammed's wise course, and
    made the *St. James's* your " mountain."
I hope you didn't dream to find all your old boys
    stelligerent chieftains ?
Remember that He who records the aims and
    the efforts of duty,
May write the " high private's " as high on the page
    of desert as his general's.

Howbeit, we all, great and small, low and lofty,
    rejoice in your presence,
Whatever, dear Alma, the cause that has brought
    you again unto Gotham.
We welcome you, all, heart and soul, and glowing
    with filial emotion,
Take pride in the pride you must feel in the fame
    of your peerless Justinian ;
Take pride in your matronly pride to lean on the
    arm of your Howard,
Whereon the great Martyr oft leaned in the stress
    of the terrible conflict ;
Share your pride in the soldierly <u>son</u> whose sword
    brought the might of a legion
To Thomas, death-doomed by the foe, on the banks
    of the red Chickamauga ;
Ay, thrill with the pride of your pride to gaze in the
    eyes of your laureate,
And hold, palm to palm, in your own, the hand that
    had writ *Thanatopsis ;*
To think how your pupil had come to be so suc-
    cessful a Grecian,
That Homer had learned from his lips to sing in
    such glorious English,
He couldn't tell which to prefer, his own or the
    tongue of his tutor;
Then mark how he carried his years, as if but the
    down of a thistle,
And, patting his white locks, exclaim : " How meet
    for the evergreen laurel ! "

HAPSBURGH'S RAMPARTS.

FROM THE GERMAN OF KARL SIMROCK.

IN Aargau, from a frowning height,
    A castle mocks the cannon's might ;
Who bade it crown
A steep that on the clouds looks down ?

The cost was Bishop Werner's care ;
Count Radbot's task to plant it there :
Not large, but strong,
The Hawksnest perched the crags among.

The bishop came and viewed the pile,
And skaking his gray locks the while,
Said : "Count, no wall
Nor rampart have we here at all ! "

" What matters that ? " the count replied ;
" God's temple, Strasburg's crowning pride,
Was built by you,
But wall nor bastion has thereto ! "

"Yet stands secure from fire and sword,
The house I builded for the Lord ;
But 'gainst *their* power,
A castle needs both wall and tower."

" Well spoken, brother ; yes, I see ;
For *such*, strong bulwarks there must be—
Grant brief delay ;
I'll have them here ere dawn of day."

And from the roused vales, far and near,
His summoned hosts at morn appear ;
And, band on band,
Around the fortress take their stand.

Then rang the count's horn from the steep,
And roused the bishop from his sleep—
"The ramparts, ho !
More magic feat what power can show?"

In fluttering wonder from his bed
The bishop to the casement sped ;
And, marshalled, sees
A host in steel-bright panoplies.

With blazing bucklers, man to man,
Stand like a wall, the count's liege ban ;
While many a knight,
High-mounted, towers in stalwart might.

"Count," smiled the priest, " heroic pride
  In walls like these may well confide !
  For naught can be
  So strong as martial loyalty."

And thus may Hapsburgh's living walls
  Forever guard its menaced halls ;
  And glorious stand
  A refuge for all German land !

WONDER.

FROM THE GERMAN OF NOVALIS.

THE mead took on a tender green,
  Faint bloom about the hedge was seen ;
And every day new plants appear ;
The air was soft, the sky so clear !
I knew not how my eyes were spelled,
Nor how that was which I beheld.

And aye the grove more shadowy grew,
As birds their vernal homes renew ;
Whence stole to me, from all sides round,
Their descant of melodious sound ;
I knew not how my ears were spelled,
Nor how that was which I beheld.

Now gushed and revelled everywhere,
Life, color, music, dulcet air ;
And all in such sweet union met,
That each, the while, seemed lovelier yet ;
I knew not how my sense was spelled,
Nor how that was which I beheld.

Then mused I, Is't a soul awakes,
Which all things thus so vital makes ;
And *will* its presence manifest
In thousand forms by Flora drest ?
I knew not how my sense was spelled,
Nor how that was which I beheld.

A new creation it must be !
Loose dust becomes a blade, a tree,
The tree a beast, the beast a man
Complete in action, shape, and plan ;
I knew not how my sense was spelled,
Nor how that was which I beheld.

As thus I stood.in wildered thought,
With pulsing bosom passion-fraught,
A charming maiden near me stole,
And captive took my sense and soul ;
I knew not how my heart was spelled,
Nor how that was which I beheld.

'The greenwood veiled us from the day ;
It is the Spring ! Love's own sweet May !
And *now* I saw, in this new birth,
That men become as gods on earth ;
And well I knew, each doubt dispelled,
How all was so as I beheld !

THE GIANTS AND THE DWARFS.

FROM father giant's castle,
  Sublime in feudal state,
Forth hied his buxom daughter
  In merriest mood elate ;
And in the vale she found, erelong,
  The oxen and the plow,
And eke the peasant who, to her,
  Seemed small enough, I trow.

Of oxen, plow, and peasant
  She made a general sweep,
And sped them in her apron
  Up to the giant's keep ;
When father giant muttered :
  " My child, what have you done ? "
Quoth she : " Just see my pretty toys !
  O my ! what lots of fun ! "

The father gazed and grumbled :
  " That's very bad, my dear !

Back with them to the furrow,
From whence you hied them here !
For if the dwarfs cease plowing,
The fields lack tilth of corn ;
We giants on the heights must starve,
So sure as you are born ! "

WHERE?

FROM THE GERMAN OF HEINE.

WHERE shall wanderer, worn and hoary,
  On his last long couch recline?
Under palms in Southern glory?
  Under lindens on the Rhine?

Shall my corse to earth be hurried
  In the waste by stranger hands?
Or on some lone coast be buried,
  Sea-dirged, in the drifted sands?

All is one!—God's heaven as brightly
  Will bend o'er me there as here;
And its stars, like death-lamps, nightly
  Watch my slumbers, just as near!

THE FIRST SONG.

FROM THE GERMAN OF BARON HOUWALD.

'ER half the globe, a minstrel guest, I'd strayed
from zone to zone,
And foreign tongues could speak and write, as
aptly as my own ;
I heard the great ones of my time, familiar, call me
friend,
And oft from thrones saw royal hands, to welcome
mine, extend.

Now on the Switzer's hoary Alps, then where Pom-
peii sleeps,
Anon beside the Pyramids, then by La Plata's
deeps—
There have I shown my lyric power, and there the
poet's verse
A thousand hearts reëcho fain, a thousand lips re-
hearse.

At length, with honor's emblem star upon my swelling breast,

The rapture of a glorious name, my bosom's con-
    scious guest,
I turned me from the alien lands tow'rd that mag-
    netic spot,
Where stood, in childhood's happy years, my long-
    forsaken cot.

And when from the last hill-top, by the old Runen-
    Mall,
I saw again my native vale, so bowery and so
    small,
With conscious pride I fondly cried : Thanks, Fate,
    miscalled the stern !
How unregarded went I forth, how glorious I re-
    turn !—

Then up the hill a woman pale, a fair child in each
    hand,
Came slowly to the turfen seat near which I chanced
    to stand ;
And resting there, a strain began, with voice so
    sweet and low,
Its pathos touched me to the heart, yet why, I did
    not know.

Then modestly I questioned her : Whence came this
    simple song ?
She answered : From the happy days of long ago,
    so long !

A young friend breathed it to his lyre to soothe
    love's parting pain—
Ah, then I fondly recognized my own, my earliest
    strain !

And farther asked I, earnest : Who gave this song to
    thee ?
'Tis known, she blushing faltered, to no one but to
    me !—
So, then, *thou* art the Mary of this young minstrel's
    spell ?
No answer.—Pray, where lives he now ?—Alas, I
    cannot tell !—

No news of him has reached thee since ?—No faint-
    est word, not one !—
Has he not written other lays ?—I know but this
    alone !—
His name ?—Ah, friendly stranger, the vain request
    give o'er !—
It may be that I know him — But *me* he knows no
    more !—

Yet, prithee, sing me once again, just once, that
    little song !—
My husband, yonder, waits for me and these dear
    ones, full long !—
And, eftsoon, in the winding lane, amid the low-
    land farms,

I saw the stranger's wife and babes clasped, clasp-
    ing, in his arms.

There stood the lofty poet, whose fame world-wide
    was flown,
A stranger in his native vale, to all but One un-
    known;
Stood, where of old he sang forlorn, yet less forlorn
    than now,
And gave to that forgotten song the garland from
    his brow!

THE SISTERS OF DESTINY.

FROM THE GERMAN OF HERDER.

CALL not Destiny inhuman ;
 Name not her allotments spite !
Her decree is truth eternal,
Clearest proof of Love supernal ;
 And Necessity, her might.

Look around, friend, keenly scanning
 All things, as the wisest may ;
What must pass, no power restraineth ;
What can stand fast, fast remaineth ;
 What must happen, happens aye !

Lovely are the fateful Sisters—
 Not, *not* Furies, wan and dire !
From their fair hands softly issues
Endless weft of magic tissues,
 For the Graces' soft attire.

Ever since sprang youthful Pallas,
 Perfect from her god-sire's brain ;

She the golden veil prepareth,
Which the starry welkin weareth
  In the æons' endless train.

And the Parcæ's gaze hangs steady,
  Fixed on their supreme employ ;
As, in worm's and angel's dower,
Faultless wisdom, goodness, power,
  Blend truth, harmony, and joy.

Therefore, call not Fate inhuman,
  Nor her stern allotments, spite ;
Her decree is truth eternal ;
Her gifts, proof of Love supernal ;
  And Necessity, her might !

THE SMACK IN SCHOOL.

ID Berkshire hills, not far away,
A district school, one Winter day,
Was humming with the wonted noise
Of three score mingled girls and boys ;
Some few upon their tasks intent,
But more on furtive mischief bent,
The while the master's downward look
Was fastened on a copy-book ;
When, suddenly, behind his back,
Rose sharp and clear, a rousing *smack*,
As 'twere a battery of bliss
Let off in one tremendous kiss !
" What's that ? " the startled master cries ;
" That, thir," a little imp replies,
" Wath William Willith, if you pleathe—
I thaw him kith Thuthannah Peathe ! "

With frown to make a statue thrill,
The magnate beckoned : " Hither, Will ! "
Like wretch o'ertaken in his track,
With stolen chattels on his back,

Will hung his head in fear and shame,
And to the awful presence came—
A great, green, bashful simpleton,
The butt of all good-natured fun.

With smile suppressed, and birch upraised,
The threatener faltered : " I'm amazed
That *you*, my biggest pupil, should
Be guilty of an act so rude—
Before the whole set school to boot—
What evil genius put you to't ? "
" 'Twas she herself, sir," sobbed the lad ;
" I didn't mean to be so bad ;
But when Susannah shook her curls,
And whispered I was 'fraid of girls,
And durstn't kiss a baby's doll,
I couldn't stand it, sir, at all,
But up and kissed her on the spot !
I know—boo hoo—I ought to not ;
But, somehow, from her looks—boo hoo—
I thought she kind o' wished me to ! "

LOVE'S ATTIC IDYL.

WHEN, erst, from " keeping company,"
  To keeping house we went,
As poor in worldy gear were we,
  As rich in heart content.

Two chairs were ours, but on my word,
  One only was required,
For you my lap as much preferred,
  As I your choice admired.

Three goblets graced our dresser trim,
  But one the board supplied ;
And where your red lip kissed its brim,
  That was my nectar side.

One eve, some twelvemonth from the date
  Our wedding tablet bore,
The doctor's gig stopt long and late
  Before our anxious door.

And when at last it stole away
  Our gravely-smiling guest,

A little rosy stranger lay
  Beside your fluttering breast.

No sleep that night surprised my joy,
  Or dulled my fond amaze ;
Our first-born babe a baby-boy !
  What could I do but gaze ?

Some other strangers since have come,
  And still we've room for more ;
Don't blush—all told, the precious sum
  Is not yet half a score.

And Fortune, too, though fabled blind,
  Has found our attic nest,
And left memorials behind,
  That speak the gracious guest.

Ah, were our sands of wedded life,
  Computed as they fall,
How far its blessings, gentle wife,
  Would oversum them all !

DAME SALISBURY'S PUDDING.

 DARE say you've heard, but if not, now you'll know,
That, down East, when a colleger's pocket runs low,
He just looks about for some vocative school,
And makes for it straight as a duck for a pool.
Well, once on a time, forced by Fortune to search
For the shiners myself, having cut me a birch,
In a certain quaint district, while "boarding around,"
Cosy quarters, at last, at the Deacon's I found ;
Where the snug kitchen still, as in primitive days,
With its arm-chairs, and settles, and cordwood ablaze,
Was the heart of the home, and more comfort enshrined,
Than scores of your new-fangled parlors combined.

'Twas a Saturday eve, and, by custom antique,
Hasty-Pudding must crown the last meal of the week ;

So the great iron pot for concocting the same
Was presently hung o'er the jubilant flame,
And the goodwife, forewarned by "help's" frequent
    default,
With her own hand made sure the right quantum of
    salt.
She had scarce left the hearth when her eldest-born,
    Rose,
Bloomed in, and, all innocence, dittoed the dose,
And glided away (how the charm of the place
Seemed to vanish at once with her beauty and
    grace !)
As Sue, sweet sixteen, tripping in, followed suit,
Unawares, with a fresh supersaline salute,
And was gone like a sylph as "help" darkened the
    door,
And astonished the brine with a round handful
    more,
Then hied for the meal-tray and ladle ; whereon
I up with the near-standing salt-box anon,
And in with the whole, laughing : "There, I opine,
If this pudding's too fresh, faith the fault wont be
    mine ! "

By and by, when transferred to the white-kirtled
    board,
And each plate with a Benjamin's portion was
    stored,
Flanked with syrups of maple and patties of gold,

And milk the town-pump never uddered, behold
The Deacon said grace with the unction and air
Of a mortal scarce worthy such fit-for-gods fare ;
Then fell to, stopped short, sputtered : " Lot's wife !
    O my !
Who salted this, Martha ? "—" *I*, husband dear,
    why ? "—
" So did I, Ma," blushed Rose ; " and I," tittered
    Sue ;
" Goodness' sake ! " exclaimed " help," " why, I
    salted it too ! "
Then quoth I : " Add *me* in, for the truth to confess,
I, likewise, my friends, had a hand in the mess,
As the *air* in the salt-box my witness will be ;
For, seeing you all with its contents so free,
I followed your savory example perforce—
At Rome, you know, one does like Romans, of
    course ! "

" Well, friends," smiled the Deacon, " just taste now,
    and see
If your palates with mine don't exactly agree :
That too many cooks are as sure, in plain troth,
To *better* a pudding no more than a broth ! "

THE ROOTED SORROW.

THEY may preach as they please, smiled the
     fair Leonore,
That beauty has wings, but I find it not so—
My image still wears the same graces it wore,
    When I looked in the bridal-glass, summers ago.

The cheek of the matron perhaps may betray
    A shade less of rose than embellished the girl's ;
But the tint is as fresh, and the dimple as gay;
    As the maiden ones kissed by these glossy brown
      curls.

Thus saying, she brushed the fair ringlets aside,
    And gazed, but the smile was soon chased by a
      frown,
As her eye, in the tale-telling mirror, espied
    A strange silver thread interlacing the brown.

Anon, through her tremulous fingers she drew
    The tress in whose ambush the pale spectre lay ;
But alas, too impatient for clearness of view,
    She banished three dark hairs to one of the gray !

Again and again to the task she applies,
  Resolved her fair brow shall be rid of its shame,
Till warned to relinquish her hopeless emprise,
  Since the brown locks alone were the worse for
    her aim. .

The moral of this is to bear and forbear,
  Let time do his worst with our gardens of rose ;
Lest, seeking to root out one innocent tare,
  We wound but the flowers where it harmlessly
    grows !

TO ESTELLE.

NEVER see me more, you say !
    And worse yet, Forget me !
But pray, how can I obey,
    If the fates won't let me ?

Were primeval gloom, Estelle,
    These charmed eyes to visit ;
I should see you just as well
    Without light as with it !

Nay, to heighten your surprise,
    When you've grandly wondered ;
See you just as well sans eyes,
    As with Argus' hundred.

As for that " Forget me,"—ah !
    Prithee don't renew it !—
'Tis not in mandragora
    To begin to do it.

Image of such witching grace,—
    Love's own photographing—
Lethe's self could ne'er efface,
    Though one died of quaffing !

SOME VIEW THE WORLD.

SOME view the world with jaundiced eye,
  And see but one sad, sallow tint ;
And some, with vision so awry,
  All seems to mock them, squint for squint.

But, brother of the sickly spleen,
  This bilious reflex you may find
Less oft the tinge of objects seen,
  Than of your own discolored mind.

Just take contentment's magic glass,
  Obedient to the wiser muse,
And you shall see the sallow pass
    Into the rose's charming hues.

And you, my captious, cross-eyed friends,
  Who see all outward forms awry ;
The muse a sovereign means commends
  Their mocking lines to rectify.

Take hope's kaleidoscope, and all
  Your shivered plans and faded dreams
  Once more to perfect shape shall fall,
And glow with all their pristine beams.

WHEN I WAS RICH.

HEN I was rich—ah, doleful *When,*
So doomed to evanescence !
What strong attractions centered then
In my complacent presence !

How brightly fell the golden sands
Of careless, cloudless leisure !
How fain were fashion's jeweled hands
To feel my answering pressure !

Where'er I sauntered, hats were raised,
As if a prince were passing ;
Whate'er I said or did, was praised
As meet for highest classing.

My taste, my style, my gait, my dress
For all times, cool or sultry—
My *whole*, indeed, was nothing less
Than culture's *ne plus ultra.*

If cards went out for feast or rout,
No soul their magic slighted—
Storm, whirlwind, megrims, blues nor **gout,**
Kept home my dear invited.

They pledged my name in many a toast,
  As proud sons might a mother's :
" Whatever fate befall our host,
  He still shall find us brothers ! "

And so I did, till Fortune frowned,
  Then snapt the brittle tether !
And all my dear good friends I found
  Blind, deaf, and dumb together.

Of every tie, from first to last,
  Their memory showed no vestige ;
The glamour of my wealth once past,
  What had I left of prestige ?

My wines were drunk, my coffers drained,
  My halls and lands, another's ;
Myself my only friend remained,
  Of all that band of brothers.

Ah, well ! to each his several road,
  The false, the frail, the fickle—
Content may reap where Folly sowed,
  If Wisdom lend her sickle !

MY TAILOR AND I IN THE LATE PANIC.

ARTOR, quoth I, the suit is well enough ;
    I find no fault, with stitching, style, or stuff :
But as for this marsupial display,
What crotchet could have led you so astray ?
Are you such Rip Van Winkle of a goose
As still to dream that pockets are in use,
When Astor scarcely can with truth be said
To have the handling of a single ' red ' ?
Pockets in times like these ? sir, 'tis no less
Than wasteful and ridiculous excess ;
As who should build a many-chambered bin,
In a great dearth, to garner nothings in.
Out with your shears ! Come, man alive ! don't
        shrink,
But off with these lean sarcasms in a twink,
Whose presence, like the spendthrift's empty purse,
But serves to make the aching void still worse.
Well done ! And now, with no more fret or fuss,
That patient little bill I'll honor—thus :
" Cashier of Hades' Bank, at blind man's sight,
Pay bearer's ghost, and debit mine.   ALL RIGHT."

SOFT AND SOFTER.

ONE eve, in velvet bravery arrayed,
　　As Phil sat toying with his darling maid,
Her little buxom waist's bewitching charm
The while half-folded in his furtive arm ;
He took her dimpled hand, and, with a smile,
Stealing it gently o'er the silken pile,
Asked, in a tender silence of love-chat,
If palm e'er fondled aught so soft as that.

She archly answered : " Might I venture, pet,
I could press yours on something softer yet."
With sidelong glance of amorous mistrust
Adown the graceful neck and swelling bust,
Whose ermine cape, his daring fancy taught,
Was the coy 'something' of the maiden's thought :
He fondly sighed, to fingers' ends a-thrill :
"Ah ! dearest, do—my hand is at your will ! "
But O lost rapture !—for, no sooner said,
She gayly clapt it pat on his own head !

ALWAYS CHEERFUL.

"ALWAYS cheerful "—yes, my friend ;
    'Twas my motto from the first,
That ill luck is like to mend
    When the bad has reached the worst.

Know you not, the arc that lies
    Deepest in the rutted clay,
Is the sole one sure to rise,
    Let the wheel roll either way ?

When my questioned purse is dumb,
    Shall I whimper ?   Nay, but sing :
Let the jingling goddess come,
    Now there's room for all she'll bring !

If the merry hint she slight,
    Still I'll carol as I go :
Empty pockets are so light,
    By my fay, 'tis better so !

Then as pomp sweeps bravely by,
    Charioted in flashing state ;

Which is safer, he or I,
　Needs, methinks, but brief debate.

If a rein or axle fail,
　Or his brisk bays mock his trust,
Prithee, what an ugly trail
　He may leave along the dust !

As for love, why fret or mope
　If one charmer prove unkind ?
Surely 'twere more wise to hope
　All the sex not quite so blind.

Should my merits find them so,
　This shall make me lighter grieve :
" Coelebs ! what a world of woe
　Adam found in finding Eve ! "

"NUMBER ONE."

FOR Christ's dark Rule at last I've got
  The rendering clear and true :
Do unto others as you'd *not*
  Have them do unto you !

Owe no man anything, says Paul—
  As if *he* knew what's right !
I say, owe all you can to all,
  And keep your purse-string tight.

It's waste of substance, want of sense,
  To pity and befriend ;
What were the use of Providence,
  If men fulfil its end ?

Am I my brother's keeper ?—Who
  Will mind the risks *I* run ?—
No, let him care for number Two,
  As I for number One.

Free course to tender sympathies
  Let generous fools accord,

Who dream that their almsgiving is
  A lending to the Lord.

Who casts his bread upon the deep,
  The waif again may see ;
But I prefer my loaves to keep
  Safe under lock and key.

The starving wretch may pine and die,
  With curses on my head ;
Yet he's as many hands as I,
  Then prithee why less bread ?

No, *Self's* the sum of all the creeds
  Mankind have ever known ;
And he is lord o'er wants and needs
  Who lives for self alone !

THE DESTROYER SUPPLIANT.

AY so, no doubt—why, look you, if Macbeth
    With only *one* foul murder on his soul
Could sleep no more, though lapped in softest down,
Nor ever smile again but just such smiles
As pain enforces, or galvanic art
Wrings from the ghastly pallor of the dead ;
How should this monster, whose lorn victims far
Outnumber all the breaths he ever drew
From his first birth-gasp, hope to close his eyes
For one brief moment's slumber, or cajole
His cheek with other than sardonic joy ?
Turn where he may, his nostril cannot shun
The taint of blood in all the general air ;
And not a wind that visits him but wreaks
On his quick ear a hell of human groans.

For him whose hand first stained the shuddering
        earth
With life's most sacred crimson, never more
Was there to be or peace with outward foes,
Or amnesty of conscience from within.

Most meet it is, then, that this Cain of Cains,
Whose crimes have drenched a continent in gore
Sluiced from innumerable fraternal hearts,
Should see a foe in every human face,
In every hand a scourge, in death itself
No refuge from the Nemesis that haunts
The guilty soul through æons of despair.

While stands he lifting his red hands to heaven
For strength to consummate his awful will
On her who bore him, crowned his petted youth
And faithless manhood with her richest gifts
(To find, at last, as Agrippina found,
Herself the mother of her deadliest foe !)—
Athwart the whole broad land, from sea to sea,
And upward from the dwelling of the palm
By sunny shores and islands ever green,
To the bleak mountains, at whose snowy paps
Are nursed the infant rivers that amaze
Ocean himself with their majestic port—
From every city, village, hamlet, grange,
The voice of lamentation, day and night,
For loved and lost ones lifts its hopeless wail.
And hark ! from Europe's overcrowded realms
The moan of famished millions, from whose hands
The iron will of this grim suppliant
Withholds the means whereby in squalid dens
The meagre crust by patient toil is won.
And hark again ! the burden of that cry

His own gaunt slaves, in awful earnestness,
Press on his helpless horror : *Give us Bread !*

Oh man of blood ! oh thruster of the hilt
Into the grasp of frenzy !   God forbid
That we should curse thee for its bitter wounds ;
Remembering WHOSE is vengeance, and withal,
That they who take, " shall perish with the sword ! "

NUPER in urbe Monumentorum
   Erat conventus Intrepidorum,
Qui nominarent, manu aut ore,
Unum e pluribus, antiquo more,
Tollere sceptrum quatuor annis,
Alba quâ domus stat Jonathanis.

Multæ, reipsa, tunc erant partes
Suis faventes, multæque artes !
CASSIUS, inquit hic, MARCIUS, ille,
Noster est dux inter homines mille ;
Tertius, se judice, nullus æqualis
Gigantis esset occidentalis ;
Sæpe in ore dum erat BUCHANUS,
Inclytus cœlebs ac Pennsylvanus.

Jungitur pugna tum viribus totis,
Quisque pro suo, verbis et votis ;
Omnibus, tamen, post omnia furta,
Triduo manet victoria incerta ;·

Palmaque cara, tam viridis visu,
Cum fere adepta, abripitur risu.
Denique cunctis, nunc defatigatis
Ictibus multis receptis et latis,
Subito stella, splendidior sole,
Albis de Montibus magna cum mole
Surgens ad polum, ministrat lumen,
Undique radios spargens ut numen !

Illico omnes—En ! omen benignum !
Ecce Mars ipse ! victrixque signum. .
Sub quo bellantes certe vincemus,
Si nosmetipsos viros præbemus ;
Agmina tam profligantes Whiggorum,
Spoliis onusta Intrepidorum,
Hostium ut in exitu certaminis
Macula væ ! non erit liquaminis !

NON MARO.

NOTES.

PAGE 16.

Monument Mountain is a remarkable precipice on the confines of Stockbridge and Barrington, from whose summit all Berkshire is visible, from Greyloch on the north to Taconic in the south.

PAGE 28.

Jonathan Edwards was the second pastor of the Stockbridge Church for nearly seven years, having been called thence to the presidency of Princeton College, January, 1758. The house in which he wrote his famous treatise on the " Freedom of the Will," etc., etc., is still standing, apparently untouched by the frosts of time.

PAGE 114.

Their *Kubleh*, or the place to which they look whilst performing their holy ceremonies, is that part of the heavens in which the sun rises, and toward it they turn the faces of their dead.—*Layard's Nineveh*, Vol. I (Yezedis).

PAGE 115.

"While they were yet, it may be, about a hundred and fifty miles from the Indian town, a little before break of day, when the whole crew were in a dead sleep, one of these women took up a resolution to imitate the action of Jael upon Sisera ; and being where she had not her own *life* secured by any *law* unto her, she thought she was not forbidden by any *law* to take away the *life* of the *murderers* by whom her *child* had been butchered."—*Cotton Mather's Magnalia Christi.*

PAGE 122.

" This village (Zinzenam) has its name from an extraordinary circumstance that once happened in these parts. A shower of rain fell, which was not properly of the nature of rain, as it did not run upon the ground, but remained very light, having scarce the weight of feathers, of a beautiful white color, like flour."—*Bruce's Travels in Abyssinia.*

See also " Cloud Crystals," etc. Edited by a Lady. D. Appleton & Co., 1864.

PAGE 138.

Lines read at the dedication of the Soldiers' Monument, at Stockbridge, Mass., Oct. 17, 1866. If my memory does not err, the little town furnished twenty-eight volunteers, several of whom never returned from the terrible conflict. It was well represented also in the Revolution, both at Bunker Hill and Bennington.

PAGE 162.

Thus death reigns in' all the portions of our time. The Autumn with its fruit provides disorders for us, and Winter's cold turns them into sharp diseases ; and the Spring brings flowers to strew our hearse ; and the Summer gives green turf and brambles to bind upon our graves.—*Jeremy Taylor.*

Proem to Centennial Echoes, Lee, Mass., Sept., 1877.

When the continental march of silvan destruction, which began at Plymouth in 1620, reached this far inland valley, it must have presented a scene unsurpassed for beauty in the whole temperate zone. It seems formed on just the right scale to satisfy the taste of a lover of nature, to whom the sublime in scenery, is not an indispensable requisite to its perfect enjoyment. If to the simple inhabitants the leafy world around them ever suggested any artificial change in its conformation, they were utterly destitute of all mechanical appliances for effecting it. The landscape, therefore, remained year after year, just as it had existed for untold ages. Spring and Summer draped it, as of old, in their green mantle; Autumn, in vesture more gorgeous than ever adorned the tiring-chamber of kings; and Winter folded in its gracious ermine the latent life in death so soon to rejoice in another vernal resurrection. From lateral ridge to ridge all was one unbroken forest, save where the beneficent river had blest its dusky children with treeless intervals, to which even their destitution of the proper instrumental means could give the semblance of agricultural life.

Into this primitive solitude came our hardy ancestors some seven score years ago, bringing with them the wants and habits of civilized society; and if perchance they also brought a taste for natural beauty, it must have been smothered or quite extinguished by the hard necessities of their surroundings. For, to the pioneer, bread is especially the staff of life; and to win it from the wilderness, his axe must first dispel its "boundless contiguity of shade," and let the rain and sunshine find free access to the dark, dank soil, never glorified by the golden footprints of Ceres. So the primitive beauty of the Berkshire Hills was obliged to give place to the stern necessities of the resolute pioneers, who established in the heart of the Housatonic Valley the famous Indian Mission, of which old Stockbridge became the central point.

In the verses which I shall have the honor to read, 1 have sought to sketch merely the three local aspects above indicated : namely, the aboriginal silvan beauty; the blotches and blemishes, the rawness, roughness, and general disfigurement, of what I venture to call the STUMP AGE ; and, lastly, the loveliness that now smiles upon us from every side, as if our Alma Mater were conscious of her peerless charms. How much these may be heightened, and what new ones added, during the lapse of another century of continued improvement under the fostering care of LAUREL HILL, FERN CLIFF.* and similar associations throughout the county, the eye of imagination only can now dimly discern. When village and hamlet and isolated farm-house shall all have been touched by the wand of refined taste, our Berkshire will be so charming, that the mere thought of its coming beauty makes one feel that he was born too early, and wish, with Franklin, that he might be permitted to revisit his native land after each hundred years' slumber in its maternal bosom.

* Chartered societies for ornamenting the respective villages. They extend the public walks, and plant trees along them each season.